Dark Wood
to White Rose

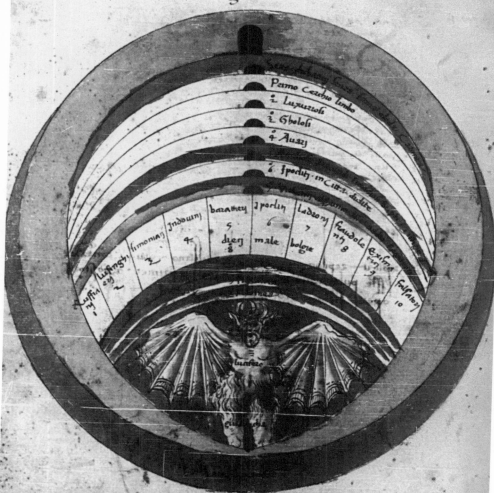

Questa fighura dello infeino non si puo poie ne dipingniere
ma spedo piano p modo che collochio chorpozale si posta uedere tudo
p pero e malta consideracio cuederlo collochio dello intellecto
secondo che perla ledeia e manifesto

Dark Wood to White Rose

JOURNEY AND TRANSFORMATION IN DANTE's *Divine Comedy*

by

Helen M. Luke

PARABOLA BOOKS
NEW YORK

DARK WOOD TO WHITE ROSE
A Parabola Book/November 1989   7/92

Illustrated edition, copyright ©1989 by Helen M. Luke
Original edition, copyright ©1975 by Dove Publications, New Mexico

Parabola Books is a publishing division of The Society for the Study of Myth and Tradition, a not-for-profit organization devoted to the dissemination and exploration of materials related to myth, symbol, ritual, and art of the great religious traditions. The Society also publishes PARABOLA, *The Magazine of Myth and Tradition.*

International Standard Book Number: 0-930407-15-6

Book Design and Production by Studio 31
Typography by Royal Type

PARABOLA BOOKS
656 Broadway
New York, NY 10012

Manufactured in the United States of America

Contents

Acknowledgment

DOROTHY SAYERS' translation of *The Divine Comedy* is used by arrangement with the agents of the copyright owner. The passages quoted were taken from the three volumes of *The Comedy of Dante Alighieri, the Florentine*, translated by Dorothy L. Sayers (Vol. III translated also by Barbara Reynolds) and published by Penguin Books, Melbourne, London, Baltimore. *Cantica I, Hell*, was first published in 1949. No copyright notice appears in the copy we drew from. *Cantica II, Purgatory*, was first published in 1955. Copyright © the Estate of Dorothy L. Sayers, 1955. *Cantica III, Paradise*, was first published in 1962, copyright © Anthony Fleming, 1962.

Preface

THROUGHOUT this study I have used the translations of Dorothy Sayers and of Barbara Reynolds, who completed the *Paradiso* after Dorothy Sayers' death. I have also quoted freely and often from their notes, and I wish to express my great admiration for their insights, without which I would never have attempted this work.

I make frequent reference to the psychology of the late C.G. Jung, to whose work I owe my basic approach to the symbolism of the poem. My abiding thankfulness for the teachings of this great man will, I trust, be obvious.

I wish to thank my friend, Charlotte Smith, most warmly for her hours of typing work so generously given.

These essays were originally written as material for study groups held at Apple Farm Community, Three Rivers, Michigan. Of my deep gratitude to my friends at Apple Farm and to all the members of our study groups here for their unfailing support and encouragement it is hard to speak. I hope they know and feel it.

Helen Luke
Apple Farm
September, 1972

Foreword

HELEN LUKE'S exploration of Dante's journey is a sensitive one. It is particularly sensitive to those points of juncture en route when the pilgrim's sense of his place in his unprecedented experience affords him access to a new level of consciousness. Her own Virgil in this endeavor has been C.G. Jung, and it is the Jungian "way of individuation"— the divided individual's recognition of division and pursuit of wholeness of being—which has provided her with a grounding for her insights. The result is a convincing meditation on the poem's pertinence to our own life's faring in the dark wood of the late twentieth century.

If today the word *individual* is commonly used to designate a particularity as opposed to a class, the dictionary advises that once upon a time a scholastic philosopher would have understood it as signifying "an indivisible unity, one in substance or essence." The thesis of *Dark Wood to White Rose* seems to me to be that what life-possibility this currently obsolete sense of the word stands for is in fact the center towards which the pilgrim's frequently faltering steps are directed, although he himself can hardly see this at the start. "At stroke of noon the descent begins," wrote Jung in "The Changes of Life." Dante's account famously commences with a crisis *mezzo del cammin*. But for the story to amount to more than a more or less patient suffering of those thirty-five years or so remaining, that is, for it to become a journey actively undertaken toward that "indivisible unity" we had certainly thought was obsolete (if we had thought of it at all), an altered consciousness is required. And this is where Helen Luke's commentary on the vital moments of transaction and transformation along the way is especially valuable.

One of the crucial features of the *Commedia* is the fact that there are two Dantes in it, Dante the poem's pilgrim protagonist and Dante the poet who has survived his epiphany and who can remember himself as he was, for example, fast asleep and scattered, on the far side of it. Helen Luke's reading of the poem's second line—

> mi ritrovai per una selva oscura

—is prompted by this double vista. *Inf.* I,2 has been variously rendered into English as "I came to myself in a dark wood" (J.A. Carlyle), "I found myself in a dark wood" (Charles Singleton), "I woke to find myself in a dark wood" (Dorothy Sayers); the author prefers the last for its approximation to the literal sense of the verb *mi ritrovai*: "I refound or rediscovered myself." From Dante the pilgrim's viewpoint, it is sufficient that he see he has lost the way he thought he was on and that he take immediate steps to find it. (In a moment he will try to, he will find himself failing, he will end up by having to put himself in the hands of something which needed his need to appear and which appears in the poem first of all in the robes of Virgil). But from Dante the poet's angle of vision, it is the dark wood itself which constitutes the initial and initiating mercy. For *per una selva oscura* means—as Helen Luke shows—not only *in* or *within*, but *through* or *by way of* a dark wood. Thus the baleful place is itself a vital part of the pattern, a means— as, soon, the three beasts on the little hill, and then Virgil, and always and finally Beatrice herself—for his process of self-recovery. Indeed, as the author glosses, "it is because of his lost state that a man is able consciously to find himself." *Sine qua non*: can there be a white rose for us without the dark wood prior? Thus the descent begins which is in truth the rising action of the journey towards wholeness which the poet Dante gives its accurate and joyful name, *commedia*.

* * *

Illustrations accompanying this edition of *Dark Wood to White Rose* have been selected from the magnificent *Illuminated Manuscripts of the Divine Comedy* by Peter Brieger, Millard Meiss and Charles S. Singleton (Bollingen Series LXXXI: Princeton University Press, 1969), a collection of iconographically and/or artistically significant miniatures illustrating the poem made from within a decade of the poet's death in 1321 up to about 1465. Illuminations and illustrations are meant to bring light, to elucidate. *PARABOLA* hopes that this selection will enrich the reader's experience both of the poem and of the essay which is here presented in its second, augmented edition.

Joseph Cary
Professor of English
University of Connecticut

Introduction

Part I

DANTE DID NOT himself call his comedy "divine"; the word was added by later publishers. It is misleading because it expresses only half of the truth, which is that the *Commedia*, while it is certainly divine, is just as certainly human. From its beginning on the threshold of Hell to its end in the vision of God, the poem resounds with the double nature of reality which is the single truth: without divinity there can be no conscious humanity and without humanity the divine remains an abstraction.

Why did Dante call his great story of the inner journey a comedy—no, not a comedy, *The* Comedy? We use the word comedy loosely to express something amusing, but in its specific literary sense, as opposed to tragedy, it means a work that has a happy ending. In a great comedy we are always made aware of the darkness in life, but the ending must be happy or it is not a comedy. A man's journey to wholeness is therefore most rightly named *The Comedy*, for the end is the final awareness of that love which is the joy of the universe. Fairy stories usually have happy endings, not because of a childish wishful thinking, but because they are true to life itself; and the man who finally refuses validity to the "happy ending" is outside the human community and has chosen to live in the monotony and meaninglessness of Hell.

The fact that the "happy ending" to a story is so often sneered at in our day is a frightening thing. It is thought of as sentimental optimism, and so very often it is, in the hands of an inferior writer or thinker; but when the potentially true poets and artists confuse this superficial concept with the intensity of meaning which may be born from the heart of tragedy, then indeed there is cause for fear, because it argues a blindness to the very nature of poetry—of the human imagination itself: to know meaning is to glimpse the joy of the end. The great poets of tragedy, such as Shakespeare and Aeschylus, never leave us with a sense of meaningless horror and disaster. Out of the darkness shines an intense ray of hope and beauty which owes its brilliance precisely to a clear-eyed acceptance of the terror of the story. To all eternity Cordelia *lives*; but to discover this we must pass through Hell itself, as Dante did to make this same discovery.

There is a widespread contempt nowadays for the belief of Christians in a life after death, in which, it is said, they take refuge from the horrors of "reality," so-called. Those who reject this belief would do well to reflect on the fact that in doing so they are guilty of precisely the same kind of unconscious projection as is the superficial Christian. Both are incapable of seeing life whole and mistake the dimension of time, and the partial truths of cause and effect, for the reality itself.

In the interior world there can be no conscious life, no true awareness whatever without a continual dying—without repeated deaths of old attitudes, of superficial desires, and finally of every claim of the ego to dominance. The fact is that life after death, or rather life out of death, is *the* truth of the universe, natural as well as psychological and spiritual, outwardly as well as inwardly. It would seem unlikely, to say the least of it, that the death of a man's individual psyche should be the one exception to this universal law. We are at liberty to imagine as we will the form of life which may emerge from the transformation experience of death; not only that, but as C.G. Jung points out in his commentary on the *Bardo Thodol* (the Tibetan Book of the Dead), it is of profound importance for a man's life in this world that he make the effort to imagine the after-death state.

In the Middle Ages, before the modern spectacular development of ego-consciousness, the collective vision filled this need for most men, whose inner life was lived in projection. It is foolish to look down on such visions, for a psychic truth is in them, however much it may be obscured by our greater factual knowledge. Through a passion for truth on one level, we are in danger of mistaking the part for the whole in a far more devastating way than did our ancestors, so that we deny the truths of the imagination, without which the "letter killeth." There are, however, many signs of a new emergence of that hope which is born of the certainty buried in the unconscious of us all.

On one of the albums by Simon and Garfunkel, there is a song called "7:00 News/Silent Night," in which the ancient carol is quietly and beautifully sung while, at first dimly, then more and more clearly and loudly, we hear the voice of a broadcaster of the news announcing dispassionately the kind of violent and terrible events to which we are daily accustomed to listen. I know that many react to this as though it were yet another image of despair—the submergence of all hope of peace and joy in the harsh violence of our day. But when I heard this song it moved me deeply in quite a different way. The voices of the singers of the ancient carol were in fact not even faintly shaken. Certainly it became easier and easier as the song drew to its close to attend only to the announcer and his message, to cease hearing the beautiful voices singing quietly and un-moved of the peace beyond understanding; but he who really attends to the wholeness of the song will feel with a surge of joy yet another promise of the light shining in darkness and hear the still small voice which speaks clearly now as it always has, no matter how loud the voices of the crowd. Whether the writers of the song were aware of the more profound meaning of their work, I do not know. But even if not, then it rose up out of their unconscious and asserted itself through them.

The disintegrating effect of "the bomb" on the young has, I believe, been exaggerated. Death from plague, undernourish-ment, massacres, and so on must have hung over our ancestors with an even greater imminence than the bomb. The disinte-grating force is not the threat of death and suffering; men have never felt safe from these things, and the response of the human spirit is clearly seen in the calm rebuilding of villages repeatedly destroyed by volcano or earthquake. The truly deadly thing is our loss of the inner certainty of the "happy ending": the meaning which we may choose, if we will pay the price, in the face of every disaster. Once a man has known this certainty through an experience, however brief, of faith and hope and love in the true sense of these words (the sense in which they are used by Dante), while it in no way reduces the horrors of war, of pollution, of all the facts of our present life, he is able to face these fearful things and fight them with all he has on one level, while abiding in peace on another. It is very certain that there is no hope at all for real change except through the awareness in individuals of the possibility of redemption into ultimate wholeness and bliss—not in some future life but here and now. It is of his own experience of bliss in *this* life that Dante wrote, but he came to it through his intense imaginative vision of the life beyond. His outer life was a long tragedy of loneliness and poverty in exile, but surely no one has ever accused him of *escaping* into imagination.

Our thinking is blinded and obsessed by a kind of worship of quantity and numbers. The bomb could kill millions; whereas the savagery of a primitive battle killed only hundreds, which, it is tacitly assumed, hardly mattered in comparison. Positively as well as negatively we fall into the same error—the success and rightness of a church, a movement, of any group is judged by the numbers of its adherents. The fever for statistics amounts to a cult; it extends even to the tabulation of mystical experiences. There is a passage in C.S. Lewis' book, *The Problem of Pain*, which can shock us out of this obsession:

> We must never make the problem of pain worse than it is by vague talk about 'the unimaginable sum of human misery.' Suppose that I have a toothache of intensity X: and suppose that you, who are seated beside me, also begin to have a toothache of intensity X. You may, if you choose, say that the total amount of pain in the room is now 2X. But you must remember that no one is suffering, 2X: search all time and space and you will not find that composite pain in anyone's consciousness. There is no such thing as a sum of suffering, for no one suffers it. When we have reached the maximum that a single person can suffer, we have, no doubt, reached something very horrible, but we have reached all the suffering there ever can be in the universe. The addition of a million fellow-sufferers adds no more pain.[1]

Each one of us is alone with his own suffering; the pain of a single man is as important and significant as the pain of a million. Our compassion is deadened, not heightened, by the continual horrors reaching our ears through the mass media. When we read of a massacre or an earthquake, we give a gasp of horror and are relatively unmoved; it is when we see a single man crushed to death that we truly suffer. This truth is of immense importance for all of us. By forgetting it we literally evade the battle with evil, for we are unable to see the murderous things we may be doing to someone in our immediate environment; while we indulge our hatreds by well-meant but empty talk about collective horrors and the wickedness of governments.

Not once in the *Commedia* are we left with a mere description of the horrors of Hell or the pains of Purgatory in a collective sense, nor invited to be stunned by the *numbers* of people who suffer. On the contrary, in every single circle of Hell and on every separate terrace of Purgatory, and just as surely, at every stage of the Heavens of Bliss, Dante meets, describes, and talks to one or two distinct *individuals*. It is because we are set face to face with unique individuals that the impact is so great, and, entering into the experience of a single soul, we recognize his suffering or his joy as an image of the hidden movements of sin or pain or bliss in ourselves.

The savagery of the poets of today in their attack on the evils of society can be matched and surpassed over and over again by passages from the *Commedia* in which Dante ruthlessly exposes the politicians and warmongers of his time. But so often the second-rate poet, or reformer, simply stops there, thus adding his mite to the very destructiveness he condemns. Evil must indeed be exposed, and denounced, and fought by word and action, but it is never conquered by mere exposure nor by the passion of rejection nor by action alone, necessary as these things are. It becomes powerless before one thing only, which is the certainty of a man who, while evading nothing of the dark facts, asserts and acts out of the joy at the heart of life. This is not cheap optimism, nor has it anything to do with superficial happiness. It is a kind of certainty that can never be born of evasion; indeed, those who do not know it are the ones who evade, for in some way they have refused or have been unable to face the conscious "journey into self."

No, the sickness of our society is not due to the threat of the bomb, to the ineptitude or corruption of the Establishment, to wars, or to the machinations of Communists or Capitalists. These evils are effects, not causes; they have always existed and are no worse because of the enormous scale on which they now operate. Our sickness is fundamentally due to the breakdown of the symbolic life which all the great religions have existed to maintain, so that we are left with eyes that see not and ears that hear not beyond the literal facts and voices of our environment. We hear *only* the dark news of the broadcaster, and our inner ear is deaf to the song of angels.

It is for these reasons that the *Commedia* is relevant to our time, more powerfully, perhaps, than to any other century since Dante's own. There are horrors in the *Inferno* which outmatch any of the evils which surround us and, as we read, we know that the way out is the way down—the journey of *one man alone* in the fullness of conscious choice down to the center of the darkness and beyond to the realization and acceptance of individual responsibility in the *Purgatorio*. Then, after the long hard climb of self-knowledge is complete, the wayfarer comes to the "happy ending" in the *Paradiso*, where he glimpses the infinitely varied vision of wholeness, of which the images are patterns of light and dance and song. No one of the three divisions of the *Commedia* makes sense without the other two, and to read one of them in isolation is to miss the point.

As we make the journey down and the journey up, meeting the shades in each of the three realms, we must never forget that our final concern is with Dante, the living man, who will return to ordinary human consciousness, and for whom, as for us, the darkness of the pit, the clarity and hard work of purgation, and the intuitions of bliss are simultaneously present, consciously or unconsciously. At the moment of supreme consciousness, which Dante describes in the last canto of his poem, all of them are there in their total meaning, when, beyond up and down, dark and light, he sees the entire universe in the Center, and finally in a flash of awareness, knows the truth of incarnation—nature, humanity, and God as one.

Every great artist, using the idiom of his own time but moved by his intuitive awareness of the unchanging realities of the psyche rising from the well of the unconscious, speaks in images which convey the truths of being to men of poetic vision in all ages, though their idiom may be completely alien to his. I would emphasize also the truth that the work of all great artists awakens insights and meanings of which the artist or writer is himself unconscious. In tracing our own "way of individuation," in Jung's terminology, through the medieval imagery of Dante's poem, we must, however, beware of trying to force his imagery at all points to fit our own. Charles Williams (*The Figure of Beatrice*) said that Dante had the genius wholly to imagine the Way to the vision of God "after a peculiar manner indeed, but then that is the nature of the way of Images. If a man is called to imagine certain images, he must work in them and not in others."[2] The great mistake of the exponents of one universal religion (or one brand of Christianity, for that matter) is that, in trying to make all ways the same on the wrong *levels*, they effectively kill the intensity of all the gloriously different approaches, and so the real unity underlying them all is lost in a kind of collective drabness.

The great danger of a psychological approach to a work of art is that it may kill the poetry; in which case such an undertaking is worse than meaningless. So let us remember as we travel with Dante that, while we may search out the extraordinary richness of his psychological wisdom and translate it into our own language, yet we must never tamper with his imagery. It will speak to us in its own terms or not at all. If, however, we can open our inner eyes and ears so that we feel the tremendous impact of this unmatched outpouring of living images, then indeed we may know a stirring to new life of our own crushed or dormant capacity for image-making, by which alone facts may grow beyond themselves into truth, and action be transformed into the movement of love.

PART II

There are in the *Commedia*, as is well known, four levels of meaning, defined by Dante himself in a letter to his friend and patron, Can Grande della Scala. He speaks of the outer, literal level and of the three-fold inner significance of the poem— allegorical, moral, and anagogical or mystical. As for the historical facts, they need concern us little here. A good and simple commentary, such as that of Dorothy Sayers, tells in a few words enough of the background of the images to give the associations from which our imagination may take wing.

The allegorical in its strict sense, as distinct from the symbolic, also has little to say to us, and, we may be tempted to think, it has a minor importance for Dante himself in spite of a few benighted critics who have seen Beatrice as simply and solely an allegorical figure standing for Theology. There are only two episodes which are strictly and avowedly allegorical, and Dante makes it clear that these are in the nature of masques or mimes, such as were common in the Middle Ages, inserted into the action. These are the two processions of allegorical figures in the Earthly Paradise. Nevertheless, at the center of the pageant of the Sacrament, in which Beatrice stands for the Sacrament itself, there comes one of the most vividly and poignantly human episodes in the whole poem— Dante's personal meeting with Beatrice and her rebuke. There could be no more powerful reminder that the Sacrament is not an allegory, but is known to each one of us through his own unique "God-bearing image" (Charles Williams' phrase) at the heart of human relationship.

The two levels of the poem which speak to us today with all of their original force, and more, are the moral and the mystical or symbolic. I hear voices exclaiming that, while the symbols may have something to say to us, surely the rigid moral codes of the medieval church are out of date. The answer is that Dante's understanding of the true nature of morality went far beyond a superficial acceptance of codes, penetrating to the realm of those inner choices in the individual soul without which no degree of aesthetic appreciation or emotional experience of symbols has any meaning. The Church has, to its undoing, held too long to the outer moral imperatives which were a necessity for unconscious men, and its leaders would do well to listen again in depth to the voice of one of the greatest of her sons. But at the other end of the scale, the apostles of the individual mystical experience as an end in itself stand in even greater need of Dante's moral wisdom. The man who wrote the last canto of the *Paradiso* knew that we can never come to this vision by any shortcut. We cannot bypass the experience of Hell; and still less can we evade the long struggle of Purgatory, through which we come to maturity in love.

Dante built his narrative on the framework of the medieval theories of life after death, but it is first and foremost the story of his own journey in this life from the "dark wood" of his lost innocence, where he wanders in blindness and near despair, to the clear vision of the heavenly rose, and his glimpse of that "love which moves the sun and the other stars." It is a tremendous symbolic account of the "way of individuation," which is the name given by C.G. Jung to this same journey. As we read the last famous line and close the book, we are left with an overpowering feeling of awe at the *completeness* of the poem. There are poets who bring alive for us the beauty and ugliness of this world, and there are those who penetrate the heights and depths of the emotions; in others clarity of intellect and penetrating thought shine through their verse into our minds; and yet others open to us through their intuitive vision the elusive country of the Spirit. But only the greatest of the great do all four of these things. Dante's journey is the bringing to consciousness of them all into one great patterned whole. He is both extrovert and introvert; neither the outer nor the inner world is exalted at the expense of the other. Each function shines out, its beauty enhancing the splendor of the others. In the heights of the *Paradiso*, beyond the natural world, we are still rooted in the sights and sounds of every day through a sudden vivid image of the market place; and the most intensely reasoned of the philosophical discourses are never wholly dry, even when our heads protest, because Dante, and we with him, are constantly aware of the personality of the one who speaks—and feels as he speaks.

Sensation, intuition, feeling, this and that, matter and spirit, all derive from the Love that moves the universe; and although these things are split apart and war with each other in fallen man, yet nothing he ever thinks or feels or does is moved by any other power than that same Love, however tragically it may be split into love and hate or displaced onto fragmented and perverted goals from its proper object, which is the whole. This is the theme of the whole poem: the conscious return of a man (and through him of the City, the Community) to the Center, which is love made whole, by the hard road of individuation. It is a road which leads through experience of the uttermost extreme of separation from that Center, and back through the long effort of discriminating every movement of our wandering loves, until, when the purging is over, we stand on the borders of Paradise. Then indeed each man's particular "Virgil" may say to him, "over thyself I mitre thee and crown."

The Inferno

The Threshold of Hell

DOROTHY SAYERS wisely stressed that by far the best approach to the poem is to read it through for the first time purely as a story, an exciting adventure story, not bothering about explanations of obscure passages, intricacies of medieval cosmology and so on. We are carried through by the plot, by our love and interest in the characters, and by the radiant beauty of the poetry which reaches us even in translation. Then there may come for many of us a second reading in which each may journey in a deeper way, seeing in this or that incident an image of his own experience on the way, memories of the past, vivid images of present struggles, and glimpses of the path he may tread in God's good time.

It is not my purpose to go through the *Commedia* step by step in detail, but rather to trace some of the "movements of love" through each of three states of consciousness, as Dante experiences them, particularly in the recurrent vital moments of transition along the way. Each of these moments or gateways admits him to a new phase of consciousness, a new depth of experience, and in the life of every man it is the same. Often we sense that we have arrived at the threshold of such a gateway, which is still closed to us. What are we to do? Sometimes we must storm the gate, sometimes consent to a great risk; sometimes we are carried through by another, sometimes we must exert every faculty of mind and heart; and sometimes we must simply wait for the moment of its opening. Dante does all these things on the many thresholds of his poem until he reaches the gateless gate of the end.

The threshold of the entire journey is the dark wood of the beginning. A man arrives there usually, but not by any means always, at the midpoint of life. Dante was 35 in the year 1300, the date he assigns to the journey. It may come later; and often, especially nowadays, it comes much earlier—the moment when we awaken to know that we are lost—to realize, as Jung says, that the ego is not master in the house, that we are stumbling around in the dark, and that our complacent goals of power, success, respectability, rebellion, uplift, or a thousand others are empty and meaningless. It is a moment of great fear—a fear ". . . so bitter it goes nigh to death."

The most famous, perhaps, of all Dante's images is this dark wood. Here are the first lines of the *Commedia*:

Nel mezzo del cammin di nostra vita
mi ritrovai per una selva oscura
che la diritta via era smarrita

Ahi quanto a dir qual
era è cosa dura
esta selva selvaggia e aspra e forte
che nel pensier rinova la paura!

Tant' è amara che poco è più morte . . .

Dorothy Sayers translates:

Midway this way of life we're bound upon,
I woke to find myself in a dark wood,
Where the right road was wholly lost and gone.

Ay me! how hard to speak of it—that rude
And rough and stubborn forest! the mere breath
Of memory stirs the old fear in the blood;

It is so bitter it, goes nigh to death. . . .

The words "*mi ritrovai*" do not simply mean "I found myself"; they mean, "I refound or recovered myself." Sayers has pointed to this by translating "I woke to find myself"—which is a glance forward to the words, "I was so heavy and full of sleep when first I stumbled from the narrow way." This does give the feeling of a refinding, but, like all other English translations I have seen, it conveys the correct literal meaning of a man waking up to realize that he is lost in a wood yet it does not carry us on to the intuitive glimpse of the entire scope of the threefold poem, which those extraordinarily terse six words contain. It would probably be impossible to do this in English short of many lines. For Dante does not say, "*mi ritrovai **in** una selva oscura*"—he says, "***per** una selva oscura*"—and although it is perfectly correct to translate *per* by "in," the more usual and basic meaning of the word *per* is nevertheless "through" and not simply "in." The image is of a man stumbling about without direction in a dark wood, but the poet is surely also telling us in those few words that it is precisely *through* the terrifying experience of the dark wood that we find the way of return to innocence; that indeed it is because of his lost state that a man is able consciously to refind himself. To refind—in the *Isha Upanishad* it is said, "O man, remember." The coming to consciousness is not a discovery of some new thing; it is a long and painful return to that which has always been. That is why when a new insight breaks through to us we always have a sense of recognition. It is fascinating to remember that in the *Bardo Thodol*—that other great imaginative account of life after death with its totally different philosophy and imagery but profoundly similar significance—there is the constantly re-peated exhortation, "O man recognize. . . ." So, as we travel with Dante, we may recognize ourselves.

The dark wood, then, is the threshold of the whole journey, but it is also an immediate threshold to an immediate gateway, through which we must pass in a direction which seemingly leads away from our goal. Moreover, we are incapable of finding it alone. There is only one thing that can save a man in such a pass. It is to admit that he is completely lost and just how frightened he is, and to force himself to look up and away for a moment from his self-pity and absorption in the ego—in other words to affirm hope. "Then I looked up. . . ." Dante simply raised his eyes and *looked*, and at once came the blessed glimpse of a mountain pointing to Heaven; and he saw the sun, the light of consciousness, shining down upon it. Again we are given a hint of another of the great themes of the whole poem, which is "Look, look well. . . ." We are to learn an ever deeper looking with the inner eye.

At this point of realization, Dante did three things. He forced himself to look back with eyes wide open at his fear; he rested awhile; then he tried his best to climb the mountain. He wanted, as we all want, to go the shortest and the quickest way to his goal; but "*la diritta via*" of the utterly childlike and innocent is for few in any age, for the very few in ours. That it was the wrong way for him, Dante very speedily found out; but if he had not made that courageous effort to scale the mountain, simply putting one foot in front of the other in the direction which seemed to him the right one, he would never have learned his true path. He was hindered and finally turned back by three beasts—the leopard, the lion, and the wolf—by his love of pleasure, by his fierce pride, and by the terrifying

Fig. 1: Opening Pages: Inferno

latent greed and avarice of the ego. So indeed do we learn, struggling out of the dark wood, that we cannot hope to find wholeness by repressing the shadow sides of ourselves, or by the most heroic efforts of the ego to climb up, to achieve goodness. The leopard, the lion, and the wolf will not allow it, we may thank God. It is when we admit our powerlessness that the guide appears.

It is well, before we move from the threshold of the journey through the first gate, to pause for a moment and consider the nature of the guides who must be trusted and followed. To Dante there came the soul of the poet Virgil whom he had loved. This is the psychopompos within, who is usually first made conscious to us through a meeting with some actual person from whom we catch the spark and who may be, for a shorter or a longer time, the teacher—the *guru*, as he is called in India. The relationship between Dante and Virgil, however, has a very different flavor from that between guru and disciple in the East. It is thoroughly Western in its nature; he is revered master and teacher certainly, often a father to Dante in his fear and ignorance, but he is also a fellow poet, friend, and peer. There is a beautiful and subtle change in their relationship when they reach Purgatory, paralleling Dante's inner growth. Virgil remains the guide, but we feel the gradual transition from dependence to equal friendship. It is even clear from the beginning that, great as is Virgil's understanding, there is a limit to it beyond which Dante the pupil will soar into a mystical consciousness closed to the guide himself. It is a very wonderful and beautiful thing, this clearsighted knowledge on both sides; it generates a sadness without bitterness at the inevitable parting to come, but in no way does it alter Dante's love and reverence for Virgil and his total obedience; nor is there a flicker of envy to mar Virgil's severity and tenderness. In the outer story this unalterable fact is due to the "accident" that Virgil lived before Christ and was therefore shut out from the Christian heaven—a dogma which seems monstrous to our externalized thinking. Inwardly, however, as Dorothy Sayers beautifully says, it is a symbol of the truth that we are only capable of entering into those states of being which we are first capable of imagining; Jung has said much the same thing. Virgil's imagination, great though it was, did not finally pass the bounds of the collective consciousness of his time, or win the freedom beyond reason.

The true meaning of the much abused word "Imagination"

Fig. 2: The three beasts; Virgil appears

must be clearly distinguished from the kind of empty day-dreaming which is sometimes called imagination. Throughout this study I use it in Blake's sense: "That something which in its inception may be called Faith, in its maturity Vision, and in its realization Eternity, is what Blake sums up under the one term Imagination" (H. Goddard, *Blake's Four-Fold Vision*).

It is likewise an inner truth that the guiding functions which lead us through the early stages of the journey are not the same as those that will lead us at the last. Virgil is a man of reason in the best sense; his feelings also are strong and true; he is both tender and stern, courageous and wise. He it was who first awakened Dante's poetic imagination and could lead it to all but the ultimate levels of vision. So on what we may call the analytical phase of our journey, we are led by these qualities in ourselves, whether conscious, or speaking through the figures of the unconscious, or projected onto another. But there may come a time when we reach at last the top of the mountain of purging, when the guide whom we have followed thus far will be able to say, like Virgil to Dante, "over thyself I mitre thee and crown."

It might be thought that at this point a man has no further need of a guide. On the contrary, after the tremendous effort of becoming conscious, he has at last reached the point where he is able to accept with a whole heart and with fully awakened Imagination the leadership of the Self through his own unique "god-bearing image." The story of the change from the leadership of Virgil to the leadership of Beatrice belongs to the threshold of the Earthly Paradise, and I will say no more of it here; but it is important to remember that the greater guide is implicit in the lesser. It was Beatrice who sent Virgil to the rescue, and she is recognized by Dante from the beginning as the lodestar of his journey. So in every man the buried awareness of his capacity for love and relationship—his "anima," the woman within—is that which activates and brings to consciousness the true guide in both inner and outer worlds at each stage of experience. Virgil stands beside Dante and thus speaks:

> "But, as for thee, I think and deem it well
> Thou take me for thy guide, and pass with me
> Through an eternal place and terrible. . . ."
>   (I, 112–114)

And Dante replies:

> ". . . Poet, I thee entreat,
> By that great God whom thou didst never know,
> Lead on, that I may free my wandering feet. . . ."

> So he moved on; and I moved on behind.
>   (I, 130–136)

Dante, however is still upon the threshold of the way. He has not crossed it. What follows here is so familiar to all of us that it brings a sudden warm and personal feeling about Dante. We are indeed going to read about the doings of a great genius, but he is not far removed from our weak strugglings. Here is a man, like to ourselves, a *person*—and it is of course this that makes the poem a living human story which nourishes every reader's own symbolic life. For Dante never spares himself; he reveals all his weaknesses with ruthless honesty but without bitterness; moreover he can laugh at himself. On the other hand, he does not shrink through false modesty from recognizing the immensity of his achievement.

The poets had not taken more than a few steps when Dante speaks:

I soon began: "Poet—dear guide—'twere wise
Surely, to test my powers and weigh their worth
Ere trusting me to this great enterprise."

(II, 10–12)

He then describes the great virtues of those who have taken
the journey through Hell before him, and goes on:

"But how should *I* go there? Who says so? Why?
I'm not Aeneas, and I am not Paul!
Who thinks me fit? Not others. And not I.

Say I submit, and go—suppose I fall
Into some folly? Though I speak but ill,
Thy better wisdom will construe it all."

As one who wills, and then unwills his will,
Changing his mind with every changing whim,
Till all his best intentions come to nil,

So I stood havering in that moorland dim,
While through fond rifts of fancy oozed away
The first quick zest that filled me to the brim.

(II, 31–42)

"Fond rifts of fancy"—the false imitation of true imagining is
his undoing. Virgil's reply is first a sharp rebuke for "sheer
black cowardice," but this is followed by patient reassuring
words. Virgil tells Dante that in coming to guide him he did
not act on his own initiative but came at the request of Beatrice,
who in Heaven had heard from The Lady herself dire news of
his plight. His description of her words to him—our first
introduction to the image of Beatrice—are enough to banish
any illusions of her as a cold allegorical abstraction. She had
told Virgil, he explains, that a *friend* of hers was hard beset.

". . . yea, and I fear almost
I have risen too late to help—for I was told
Such news of him in Heaven—he's too far lost.

But thou—go thou! Lift up thy voice of gold;
Try every needful means to find and reach
And free him, that my heart may rest consoled.

Beatrice am I, who thy good speed beseech. . . ."

(II, 64–70)

Fig. 3: Beatrice's message to Virgil

Surely she is the archetypal feminine through which a man is linked to the deep unconscious and to the heavens of bliss, but she is also a single human friend—a unique woman loving a unique man and believing in him with all her heart. Moreover she does not express any cold moralistic motives—she simply loves him and is terribly anxious, and begs for help "that my heart may rest consoled."

Dante's black cowardice, and ours, is, like all shadow things, a bringer of wisdom when admitted and faced. It is most surely true that no man can safely enter the dark gate of the shadow world without knowing that some deeply loved and trusted *person* has absolute faith in the rightness of his journey and in his courage and ability to come through. It was a part of Jung's greatness that he understood this and insisted that, instead of hiding himself and remaining completely outside the process going on in the patient, the analyst must himself be completely involved, on another level, so that he himself was changed every time he became a guide to another on the journey. He—or she, of course—must never forget, however, that he is outer guide and friend at the bidding of the inner guide of his pupil, and it is when the pupil senses this love both personal and impersonal within his teacher that he will pass the gate into the "hidden things."

Virgil's description of Beatrice's concern does what no amount

of reason or promise of success could do, and Dante describes
it with one of his breathtakingly beautiful images:

> As little flowers, which all the frosty night
> Hung pinched and drooping, lift their stalks and fan
> Their blossoms out, touched by the warm white light,
>
> So did my fainting powers; and therewith ran
> Such good, strong courage round about my heart
> That I spoke boldly out like a free man:
>
> "O blessed she that stooped to take my part!
> O courteous thou, to obey her true-discerning
> Speech, and thus promptly to my rescue start!
> . . . .
>
> Forward! henceforth there's but one will for two,
> Thou master, and thou leader, and thou lord."
> I spoke; he moved; so, setting out anew,
>
> I entered on that savage path and forward.
>
> (II, 127–142)

Thus Dante, having found his guide, stands before the Gate
of Hell and passes through it. On the lintel he sees an inscription. I quote the first line and the last:

> THROUGH ME THE ROAD TO THE CITY OF
> DESOLATION,
> . . . .
>
> LAY DOWN ALL HOPE, YOU THAT GO IN BY ME.
>
> (III, 1–9)

To Dante's puzzled questions, Virgil replies:

> ". . . Here
> Lay down all thy distrust," said he, "reject
> Dead from within thee every coward fear;
>
> We've reached the place I told thee to expect,
> Where thou shouldst see the miserable race,
> Those who have lost the good of intellect."

He laid his hand on mine, and with a face
So joyous that it comforted my quailing,
Into the hidden things he led my ways.

(III, 13–21)

It is in this canto that Dante makes it unmistakably clear that the passing of every gateway to which we come in the inner world is a matter of individual choice. The souls in Hell are those who have "lost the good of intellect." This does not, of course, mean that it is inhabited by the non-intellectuals; it means that the damned are those who have not only fallen into the unconscious but have chosen to remain there and so lost their will to choose—which may be defined as the good of consciousness. Thus, when the poets come to the banks of Acheron, they find the newly dead pressing urgently to be carried across the river by Charon, the ferryman—and Virgil says, ". . . all their fear is changed into desire." We fear the meaningless pains of our neuroses; but at the same time, at the first glimpse of the possibility of release through responsible, conscious suffering, how often do we run frantically back to re-embrace them?

Over the gateway of Hell are the words, "Lay down all hope, you that go in by me," and it is startling to read a few lines further on Virgil's words to Dante as they pass the door, "Lay down all thy distrust. . . ." Here is the vital distinction. Hell is the abode of darkness which no man can evade. I am reminded of Jung's words to the effect that if you feel yourself falling, then the only safety lies in deliberately jumping. Dante, wandering, heavy and sleepy, in the dark wood, was in very grave danger of abandoning hope and so falling into the kind of death which is the loss of all conscious direction. He would thus have become a shade, the ghost of a human being, choosing to live in Hell. Instead he lifted his eyes and hope flowed back, and he saw and accepted his guide and through him asserted faith in the greater image of Beatrice, in the possibility of love. So, instead of falling, he jumped, consciously choosing the downward journey through the darkness; and Virgil "laid his hand on mine, and with a face so joyous that it comforted my quailing, into the hidden things he led my ways."

As we read the *Commedia*, it is clear from first to last that there are three qualities or "virtues" that are vital in the quest

Fig. 4: The Gate of Hell

for consciousness. These are the so-called theological virtues of Faith, Hope, and Love (which have nothing in common with blind belief, optimism, or personal desires). The "oughts" and "ought-nots" of moralism derive their only significance from their reflection or distortion of these three in each individual. To take a momentary jump forward and up to the eighth heaven, it is there, on the last threshold of Dante's journey, that he is examined by the three great sages and must prove his understanding of the true inner meaning of Faith, Hope, and Love before he can pass beyond time and space to his final realization. When we come to that threshold, we will study Dante's answers. Meanwhile, here at the very beginning, we are shown that he cannot take a step without at least an intuitive awareness of these three states of being.

There is one more image here, just inside the gateway of Hell, which belongs in a sense to the threshold. Here Dante meets the souls of those who have refused to make any choice at all, even the choice of giving up choice. They do not ever cross the river into Hell proper. They are the futile, the self-pitying, the sitters-on-the-fence. They are stung by wasps and hornets and they run wildly about making horrible noises, groaning and shrieking and clapping their hands without cessation. They have made no individual impression at all on the world, have simply evaded both praise and blame, running always with the crowd—clapping and agreeing or shrieking and complaining according to the mode of the moment. As Dante watches, a flag or standard is raised, and all with one accord run frantically after it. Their thinking still functions, but, being totally collective and unrelated to the choices of the heart, it is quite empty of meaning. To him they are more contemptible than the damned, many of whom have dignity and compel a kind of respect. Even Hell itself, says Virgil, rejects these souls. They can neither live nor die.

> "This dreary huddle has no hope of death,
> Yet its blind life trails on so low and crass
> That every other fate it envieth.
>
> No reputation in the world it has,
> Mercy and doom hold it alike in scorn—
> Let us not speak of these; but look, and pass."
>
> (III, 46–51)

Here Dante does indeed speak of the enormous numbers:

> It never would have entered in my head
> There were so many men whom death had slain.
>
> (III, 56–57)

He mentions just one whom he recognized, probably a Pope, who made what Dante calls "the great refusal." He was elected and resigned soon afterwards. The great refusal, then, is the refusal of one's unique fate, whether it be a Pope's or a garbage collector's. It is so much easier to run after a "standard."

There is no need to stress the immediacy and relevance of these images. We can all recognize them in the present, all-pervasive "isms" and mass ideologies, of both old and young;

it is, however, still more important that we recognize the very frequent inroads of this deadly futility or refusal of responsibility in our daily encounters. Thus perhaps we are shocked into seeing clearly for a moment in these shatteringly contemptuous images just what it is that threatens us.

Dante saw and passed on and was carried across the river into the circles of Hell itself.

The City of Dis

THERE ARE NINE circles in Dante's Hell, as there are nine terraces on the Mountain of Purgatory and nine spheres in Heaven. In each Cantica there is also a tenth region: the vestibule of the futile in the *Inferno*, the Earthly Paradise in the *Purgatorio*, and the Rose of the center in the *Paradiso*.

In Hell itself there are three main divisions. The upper five circles contain first the shades of the inadequate, then the incontinent and the self-indulgent, those who have succumbed to the gay leopard of the poet's vision in the dark wood. In the second division, the sixth and seventh circles, dwell the violent, who have identified with the fierce bestiality of the lion; while in the third pit of the eighth and ninth circles are those who have become devouring wolves. The eighth circle is the place of the deliberately fraudulent and malicious; and, finally, in the ninth, the coldly deliberate traitors and betrayers lie frozen and immobile forever in the lake of ice which is the ultimate denial of life and love. There are also numerous subdivisions in the different circles, but only three major gateways or transition points, barriers of immense danger, whose passage no human strength alone can compass. Two of these gateways divide the realms of the beasts—the leopard from the lion, the lion from the wolf. The third barrier is the entrance to the final pit of the traitors and of Satan himself.

Dante does not in fact talk specifically about the three beasts after his vision of them at the outset of his journey, but the archetypes they symbolize are implicit and clear for us to recognize all along the way, and not only in the *Inferno*. There we see what happens when they swallow us; on the mountain of Purgatory we watch them in process of transformation through the battle for wholeness. Finally in the spheres of Heaven the forces they symbolize shine out redeemed into primal innocence; for there we encounter first the joy which is the grace and gaiety of the leopard (the Moon, Mercury, Venus); then the strength and royalty of the lion (the Sun,

Mars, Jupiter); and at last the detached love into which the cold hate of the wolf may be transmuted (Saturn, the Fixed Stars, the Primum Mobile). Here the wolf is hungry no longer, for when man's love is made whole he finds eternal nourishment not only for his spirit but for his instincts also. The wolf, as he is often the most despised and feared of beasts, in fact and in legend, is also the most honored. Those who know him well tell of his intelligence and noble qualities, of his loyalty to the death, giving the lie to his evil reputation. In myth and in fact, he alone among the animals will adopt and nourish a human child. It was in the form of a white wolf that Merlin carried the new-born Galahad, the holy child, to safety.

The three beasts of the *Commedia*, then, are not left behind when Dante emerges from Hell; but there in the darkness he must first learn how deadly is the nature of those great instinctual forces, when men either despise them or identify with them.

The first circle, however, is not a place of torment, and no sinners are found there. It is called Limbo, a word which we often use to express a condition of arrested development. Here dwell the great pagans in a pale light without suffering but without joy; and surely here, as Dorothy Sayers says, live all the sincere humanists and those who have been unable to imagine bliss. Limbo, in fact, is just like the Elysian fields imagined by the ancient world and resembles a state of human well-being forever extended.

The poets then traverse the circles of the incontinent, the lustful, the gluttonous, and the angry, passing among the shades of those who were lost through irresponsibility and a

Fig. 5: The virtuous pagans

half-conscious surrender of will. Thus each of us, beginning to look at his shadow, will uncover one by one the instinctive reactions which are normal and beautiful in themselves, as the leopard is beautiful even when he kills his prey, for that is his nature. We, however, since we are human, if we either repress these instincts or indulge them, will be invaded and corrupted insidiously from within so that little by little we abandon the necessity for discrimination and finally the will to choose. The traveler with Dante will find himself forced from the very beginning to evade nothing of the ultimate implications of his smallest and most forgivable reactions when they are allowed to breed in the dark.

In the famous passage about the lovers, Paolo and Francesca, in the second circle, the poet shows them forever bound to each other, drifting aimlessly on the infernal wind. Their sin lay, not in the formal breaking of a moral law, but, as Charles Williams so beautifully put it, in their refusal of the responsibility of adult love. They *drifted* half-consciously into an adolescent passion, when offered the opportunity of mature choice; thus together they drift forever without growth. We could say that they settled for a permanent projection of "anima" and "animus" respectively, refusing the offered pain of individual choice. They are rewarded with the thing they sought—eternal identification with each other, together with the opposite of what they sought, a drifting without passion on the cold and meaningless wind.

It is not difficult to admit to these universal human weaknesses, to feel sympathy and pity, as Dante did, for those, including ourselves, who fall from desire into lust, from enjoyment of good things into greed, from spontaneous anger into half-conscious cruelty. There is so thin a line between these things, and we do not want to know when we cross it; nevertheless, in admitting to our falls, we are not yet in much danger of discouragement and probably feel much relieved at having cleared away false guilt. But with Dante now we can come to another gateway—one which is not wide open as is the gate to the upper hell of indulged or rejected instinct.

Dante and Virgil are carried by boat across the marsh of the river Styx, where the wrathful lie fighting each other in the mud, and come in sight of the great iron battlements of the City of Dis (a classical name for the underworld), which guard the entry to lower Hell. Here sin is not weakness indulged but perverted choice.

Fig. 6: The carnal sinners

These terrible walls are manned by fierce demons who cry out in a fury of protest at seeing a living man in this place of death; they invite Virgil to enter the city but contemptuously tell Dante to find his way back if he can. Dante is terrified, thinking for a moment that Virgil will desert him, so weak is his faith as yet.

> "O Master dear, ...
>
> If we may not go forward, pray let's quit,
> And hasten back together with all good speed!"
>
>> (VIII, 97–102)

Virgil, though reassuring him and confronting the demons, is himself cast down and turns pale when all his reasoning and his authority are powerless to move the gatekeepers. Then the three Furies with their terrible snakes appear on the battlements and threaten to uncover the Gorgon's Head. Virgil quickly orders Dante to cover his eyes with his hands and places his own hands over them too. If a living man catches the smallest glimpse of this horror there can be no rescue, not even from Heaven itself; he would be turned irremediably into stone.

Virgil knows they cannot move on without divine help. The humanist, however great a poet he may be, is powerless in such a pass. They can do nothing but wait, eyes covered, and hope. Then comes

A sound like the sound of a violent wind, around
The time of opposing heats and the parched weather,
When it sweeps on the forest and leaps with a sudden bound. . . .

(IX, 67–69)

Fig. 7: Phlegyas; the wrathful and the sullen

Virgil looses Dante's eyes and he beholds the messenger from Heaven, walking over the Styx with "unwet feet." Furies and Gorgon's Head have vanished at his coming.

> . . . He stood beside
> The gate, and touched it with a wand; it flew
> Open; there was no resistance; all stood wide.
>
> (IX, 88–90)

Virgil and Dante pass freely through into the circles of the violent.

What is this moment of transition on the journey towards self-knowledge? Dante's images leave one in no doubt of the terror of this threshold, of the very great danger that we meet there, and of the powerlessness of reason or courage or any noble human virtue to open the door. The gate at the beginning of the journey down is wide open; anyone can walk through it when he so chooses; but the iron walls of the City of Dis are another matter. They are thrown wide to the already damned— that is, to those who have chosen to give up the "good of intellect"—but to penetrate the darkness beyond in full consciousness is a thing no man can do without disaster, so long as he trusts in his own ego-strength alone.

Fig. 8: The approach and entry into Dis

Fig. 9: The approach and entry into Dis

It is, in some sort, we may say, the gateway between the personal and the collective unconscious. I am reminded of Jung's dream, which came to him when he was about to make his great plunge into the depths, and in which he and a small primitive man killed Siegfried. He says in *Memories, Dreams, and Reflections* that on awakening from that dream he had an overpowering feeling that it was a matter of life and death for him to understand it—that if he could not do so he would be compelled to kill himself. Then it came to him that he had to "kill," to abandon completely the Siegfried attitude, if he were not to be broken and overwhelmed by his descent into the darkness of the unconscious. Siegfried in the legend was arrogantly confident and so invited the knife in his back. Thinking to conquer and mold the forces of the unconscious to his will, Jung himself would most probably have been psychically "killed." In the imagery of Dante, he was in great danger, as he stood on this threshold, of looking upon the Gorgon's Head; and so he would have turned to stone, his humanity lost in the coldness of insanity, or despair or uncontrollable inflation. The gate of Dis can only be safely passed by those who have come to the kind of faith and humility which brought the angel to Dante's aid. This Jung knew the moment he understood his dream. The Siegfried attitude must be wholly renounced, not simply put aside; the conquering hero in all his beauty and strength must now die, for his task is done; inside the City of Dis his strength would spell disaster, not victory. Jung was moved to great sadness at his passing, as all men must mourn at this moment when the bright vision of so much that is noble in man's ego must be sacrificed if we are to enter the darkness from which the greater vision is born.

The Furies are of deep significance too. The Eumenides, the three ghastly sisters with snakes in their hair who pursue a murderer and drive him to despair, are the symbols of that deadly kind of remorse which makes any true repentance impossible; for repentance means the abandonment of all self-pitying guilt feelings in order that we may turn and face the dark truth. Any man who dares to cross the threshold of Dis and look upon the naked evil of which he is potentially capable must first break free from these three sisters before he can begin to learn the nature of real repentance. Macbeth, falling under the spell of the witches, refusing to confront them, was forced to live out the evil he looked upon. Those who succumb to the Furies, wallowing in remorse, in perpetual flight from repentance, are indeed in Hell. Jung expressed this great danger of the meeting with the deep unconscious when he said that, when a man becomes aware of the darkness within, he may easily identify his ego with the devil himself and so fall into despair. When despair of this kind is in complete possession of a man, he looks upon the Gorgon's Head and is turned into stone. The human personality must be clearly discriminated from both angel and devil before opening this door. To do this, as has been said, we must know both humility and faith, as Dante did before the gates of Dis, as Jung did before his plunge into the unconscious. Until we have this kind of strength, the Furies mercifully bar the way. How clear an image this is of the fact that the archetype works to bless or damn a man according to his basic attitude to the journey! Those who choose Hell are welcomed by the Furies, but those who are struggling towards individuation are forced by them to wait for the coming of the angel.

To go back a step, there is another incident which belongs to the threshold preparation for the entry to lower Hell. As the poets are crossing the marsh of Styx, Dante sees the soul of Filippo Argenti, a man of very violent temper whom he has known in Florence.

And as we ran the channel of the dead slime
There started up at me a mud-soaked head,
Crying: "Who art thou, come here before thy time?"

"Tho' I come," said I, "I stay not; thou who art made
So rank and beastly, who art thou?" "Go to;
Thou seest that I am one who weeps," he said.

And I: "Amid the weeping and the woe,
Accursed spirit, do thou remain and rot!
I know thee, filthy as thou art—I know."

(VIII, 31–39)

And Virgil

   . . . laid his arms about my neck
And kissed my face and said: "Indignant soul,
Blessed is the womb that bare thee. . . ."

(VIII, 43–45)

To our minds, steeped in the often sentimental tolerance of
prevailing attitudes ("Poor fellow! He is not responsible—his
upbringing or the state of society is to blame," etc.), this
passage is quite a shock, and Virgil's pleasure almost offen-
sive. Dante has hitherto shown no such reaction to the damned.
He has pitied rather then condemned. But the wrathful have
themselves denied pity. I quote Dorothy Sayers' admirable
comment:

> Up to this moment Dante has only wondered, grieved,
> pitied, or trembled; now, for the first time, he sees (in the
> image of the damned soul) sin as it is—vile, degraded,
> and dangerous—and turns indignantly against it. For what-
> ever inadequate and unworthy reasons, he accepts judg-
> ment and places himself on God's side. It is the first
> feeble stirring of the birth of Christ within the soul, and
> Virgil accordingly hails it with words that were used of
> Christ Himself.[3]

Without this acceptance of "judgment," a man may not safely
enter Dis at all. It is a matter of the discrimination of levels.
"Judge not that you be not judged" is an absolute essential for

a man's fundamental attitude towards his fellow human be-ings; but when we come face to face with the dark side of reality and look upon evil itself, there is no room at all for any easy tolerance or for a cold intellectual acceptance of the philosophical or psychological meaning of these things. It must be remembered that the souls in Hell represent *chosen* evil. Openly and clearly we must proclaim ourselves on the side of the light. Only so can we dare to look upon the opposites and move towards the final unity. We sense Virgil's great relief at Dante's outburst.

This is an insight of which we are in desperate need today. The breakdown of the old moral imperatives and their repres-sive effects is producing not only a violent upsurge of the other side, but a kind of weak permissiveness which creeps into every ramification of our society and invades even the most sincere people of good will. In the schools, for instance, well-meaning teachers, who truly sympathize with and understand the demands of the young, confuse the need for change with a complete abandonment of discrimination and a wholesale overthrowing of discipline and courtesy, of values which are the meaning of humanity itself. In families everywhere we see the same thing. Every kind of rude and inconsiderate behavior is accepted as a "need" of the growing child—while often harshness and repression are shown on issues where tolerance and love are the answer. We must accept, as Dante did at that moment on the marsh, the responsibility of discrimination, or judgment, and so find the courage to stand by the fundamental values of human relationship as we see them, however inade-quate we may be in our immaturity. It may seem that this is a contradiction of what was said above about the necessity of giving up the ego's claim to manipulate life. It is, of course, an entirely different thing, this clear discrimination of values, and has nothing to do with bending things to our will. To take a simple example, the parent who insists on courtesy is not trying to bend the child for selfish purposes. He is standing by his own values, and thereby in the long run gives the child a far better chance of finding his own. This kind of integrity applies to all our relationships, friendships, loves. Without this decisiveness in the service of the Good, as distinct from relative good, let no man pass the gates of Dis. The permissive man, as surely as the arrogant, will in the end *become* that which he looks upon in the depths.

It is a paradox. Dante, by asserting himself, showing the

right kind of anger in the circle of those possessed by anger, proved that he had the strength to let go of his belief in the adequacy of his human reason and personal strength. Jung, by killing the heroic Siegfried attitude, was able to enter the deep unconscious with an open mind. In both cases this meant the taking up of the responsibilities of judgment *and* at the same time the abandonment of the ego's claim to supremacy in the psyche. Having confronted the personal shadow, both men were ready to accept the Angel—the messenger, the intuition from the journey's end—who opens the door of Dis and lifts from the traveler both the shadow of despair and the "hubris" of the ego.

> . . . So we stirred
> Our footsteps citywards, with hearts reposed,
> Safely protected by the heavenly word.
>   (IX, 103–105)

The Great Barrier

THE FIRST IMAGE encountered by the poets as they enter the circles of the violent is the Minotaur—that horrible distortion of nature born of the mating of a woman with a bull. The creature thrashes about in a senseless fury when he sees them, and they must slip past him when he is not looking. He is a fitting symbol of that which happens to the human being who sinks half-consciously from a seemingly harmless incontinence and forgivable weakness into a state of possession where he becomes half-man, half-beast. He has scarcely noticed the gates of Dis, wide open to receive him.

All kinds of human violence spring from the blind mingling of the bestial with ego-consciousness, from the refusal to relate objectively to the instinctive forces within. The woman mates with the bull; the creative receptivity of the feminine principle, when it has turned either to weak permissiveness or to the pursuit of power, is incapable of receiving the seed of the human spirit and is penetrated instead by the mindless power and aggressiveness of the bull, the instinctive male. The relevance of the "sins of the lion" to the present sickness of our society is obvious.

Just as Pasiphae believed that the white bull was a god and that her child would be divine, so nowadays we sense under many guises this same pseudo-religious delusion: if only we are permissive enough and follow the instincts wherever they may lead, we shall somehow or other give birth to a new world in which the lion shall lie down with the lamb and all the horrors into which the repressive authoritarian way of life had led us will be swept away. This is simply to worship the underside of the god of technology and puritanism—his polar opposite—and it is so dangerous because it is *true* that the bull and the lion must be respected and loved—set free to be themselves. But if Adam does not retain his dominion over the inner beasts of the field, Eve will start *mating* with them, and then indeed the child that is born is a raging monster driving men into senseless violence, both physical and psychological.

Fig. 10: The Minotaur

Having looked upon this truth, Dante is ready to learn discrimination between the different manifestations of the Minotaur in the psyche—in his own depths. He meets souls whose violence was projected against their fellow men, and suicides who were violent against themselves; on burning sand, under a rain of fire, he sees blasphemers, sodomites, and usurers who were violent, respectively, against God, nature, and art. Blasphemers, in our language, are those who deny reality to anything beyond ego-consciousness, and so play God in their environment. Sodomites typify the people for whom the flesh, nature itself, is a thing to be used for pleasure or profit, its creative essence despised. And usurers are those who do the same thing with the products of human labor and skill. All these "turn to weeping what was meant for joy" (Canto XI, 45). Dorothy Sayers refers to an old commentator, called Gelli, who observed that the sodomites and usurers are classed together because the first make sterile the natural instincts which are created fertile, while the second make fertile that which by nature is sterile—that is, they "make money breed." Every means of exchange, actually even a manifestation of love, is sterile when it is sought as an end in itself, breeding only a repetition of itself; and everything in these circles of the violent conveys an atmosphere of sterility. The Minotaur has no issue— the awful frustration which comes when the feminine values of feeling succumb to emotional power-drives can have no other outlet but destructiveness.

Fig. 11: The Harpies

The reaction today against empty intellectuality and puritanical repression is an uprush of the values of nature and instinct. It can be a movement of great beauty and truth, or it can breed a worse form of the violence it condemns; the issue hangs in the balance and depends on those who can discriminate the truth of feeling relatedness from uncontrolled affect and are willing to make the enormous effort and the painful sacrifices which this involves. Shall we breed minotaurs or free men and women? Here in the *Inferno* with Dante, we are brought face to face with this horror—that every time we use people, our-

Fig. 12: The sodomites

Fig. 13: The usurers; descent on Geryon

selves, nature, things or concepts, however lofty, for profit or empty pleasure, to relieve frustration or to evade truth, we sterilize all creation and run aimlessly on the burning sand, or sit despairingly under the rain of fire. How powerful an image it is that the usurers are the lowest of all in these circles of the violent! They are the cold plotters of camouflaged violence and are therefore found on the very threshold of the pit of fraud. It is not to be thought that they are simply the people who lend money at exorbitant interest. We are usurers whenever we make demands upon others as a return for our actions or gifts; whenever we say or subtly feel that we are *owed* something by a person or by life itself. Before he could descend into the pit of fraud, Dante had to encounter this truth. Only then could he look upon the face of conscious, malicious deceit.

The "Great Barrier" consists of a tremendous waterfall pouring down on all sides of the circular cliff. There is no possibility of descent on foot. A curious image follows: Virgil orders Dante to give him the rope girdle he wears round his waist, and coiling it up neatly he throws it over the rim of the pit as a kind of signal. It is quickly answered; a strange and horrible beast rises up from the depths, and clings to the edge. It is the monster called Geryon, and Dante calls him "that unclean image of Fraud" itself. He has the face of a good, just man, with a mild, benign expression; his paws are a beast's, his body is reptilian, beautiful with rainbow colors, and his tail is like a scorpion's tipped with poison. On the back of this creature, held fast in Virgil's arms, Dante descends to the circles of fraud.

> No greater fear, methinks, did any feel. . .
>
> Than I felt, finding myself in the void falling
> With nothing but air all round, nothing to show,
> No light, no sight but the sight of the beast appalling.
>
> And on he goes, swimming and swimming slow,
> Round and down. . . .
> > (XVII, 106–116)

The monster had no wings; it swam in the void.

There have been various speculations about the meaning of the rope girdle, but Dante himself gives the clue. He says:

> I was wearing a rope girdle, the same wherein
> I once, indeed, had nursed a fleeting hope
> To catch the leopard with the painted skin. . . .
> > (XVI, 106–108)

If we take this, together with the fact that a rope girdle is worn by monks as a symbol of their vows, it is clear that Dante, like most of us, had attempted at one time to "catch the leopard," control his pleasure-seeking, his lusts and incontinence by means of noble, conscious resolutions. Perhaps he may even have made some kind of vow. Here he admits frankly the hopelessness of such an attempt. It is an extremely hard thing to give up finally and completely the delusion that if only we try hard enough, we will be able to alter ourselves by consciously taken decisions alone. It is in fact impossible for anyone, be he monk or layman, to do so without cooperation from the forces in the unconscious. Otherwise it is mere repression with its inevitable swing into the opposite. Dante would have been stuck here at the Barrier, unable to move forwards or backwards, if he had not been willing to abandon all remnants of this delusion. He throws all his good resolutions away; and it is this action that, so to speak, frees him from "usury" and sets him on his way, still downwards, but towards a great leap in conscious discrimination. As long as we still depend wholly on good resolutions, we remain in a usurious frame of mind. Good, we tacitly assume, is due to us because we mean well.

There is surely a hint here also of the other kind of descent into Hell, the compulsive choice of Hell as opposed to Dante's conscious exploration, for "the way to Hell is paved with good intentions." The passage from mindless violence to deliberate fraud comes about when even the good intentions, which have deluded a soul thus far down, are thrown away, and he gives himself to acknowledged evil.

The creature which is called to the surface by this throwing away of the girdle is a hideous image of what happens when good intentions are no longer even faintly sincere but have become fraudulent. The dishonest man preserves a mild and just persona, protesting innocence and integrity. The good intentions are now purely a mask; below are the sharp claws and the scorpion's tail. "We must make our faces visards to our hearts disguising what they are. . . . O full of scorpions is my mind, dear wife." Thus speaks Macbeth. Geryon has him in his claws and will carry him to the traitors' pit.

It is at the moment of throwing away the rope girdle to which we have clung that we recognize, with a shock of fear, the extreme dangers of self-deception. We see the mild and beautiful face of this monster and the glittering rainbow colors which promise all kinds of marvelous results, and look beyond them to the claws and the poisonous tail. Geryon is the gay leopard again in far more menacing form, "caught," brought to consciousness by the abandoned girdle. Once we have caught him, if we have the courage to see the true menace and will consent to be aware of our own frauds, then Geryon becomes our servant and will carry us down on his back that we may look upon the roots of evil in the psyche of man.

This matter of the rope girdle is not a mere detail; it is a major key on the way to individuation. Obviously an archetypal situation such as this is not, as a rule, a single awakening in the life of a man or woman. More often it must be encountered again and again before it is fully assimilated. Every time we are faced with a new manifestation of the shadow we are tempted to put our faith once more on the good resolution to do better next time. It is not, of course, in itself wrong; indeed conscious direction of the will is essential; but this is quite useless if we put our dependence upon it, for self-deception is always born of the confident assertion of a willed improvement. Sooner or later we must find the courage to throw away the rope girdle. Then indeed we experience to some degree that terrible fear, "finding myself in the void falling. . . . No light, no sight, but the sight of the beast appalling. . . ." Nevertheless, if we face this fear, the strong arms of the guide, the wise companion within, are around us; and the swimming beast sets us down at last beyond the Great Barrier, where we may learn the true nature of dishonesty and of ultimate betrayal, and pass beyond it to the light of day.

The Well

THE EIGHTH CIRCLE of the *Inferno* is divided into ten trenches or "bowges," as they are called, and in each of them, Dante is made aware of a different kind of malicious fraud. First he meets panderers and seducers, then flatterers, simoniacs, sorcerers, barrators, hypocrites, thieves, counselors of fraud, sowers of discord, and lastly falsifiers (who include impersonators, perjurers, and coiners). The poets look down at these shades from stone bridges which span the deep trenches, and so they come finally to the edge of the huge well at the bottom of which lie the traitors and Lucifer himself.

Malicious fraud is a comparatively rare thing. Nevertheless, those dishonesties which, if maliciously consented to, land a man in one of the bowges must be sought out and looked upon consciously in their hiding places in the unconscious lest they insidiously permeate our motives. Which of us, for example, can say that we have never manipulated the passions of others to serve ourselves, like the panderers and seducers, have never used words to exploit people, like the flatterers, or treated a holy thing as a means to personal gain, like the simoniacs? Which of us has not been tempted to manipulate the psyche of another, or to abuse some trust, or to parade some unearned merit, turning "inner truth to expedience," in Dorothy Sayers' phrase? How often do we steal energy from another, breaking into the house of his personality, invading his privacy; or secretly welcome fraud by silence or pleasure in another's sin? And the sowing of discord is something we do daily whenever we evade our own shadow and project it onto another. As to the falsifying of persons, words, and money, it is so common a thing in our society that we hardly see it anymore. Almost everyone evades the pain of loneliness by copying someone else, evading consciousness of his own truth; while few are shocked anymore by the all-pervasive prostitution of language which clouds reality and substitutes

Fig. 14: The simoniacs

verbiage for fact. As for such things as the evasion of taxes and the faking of expense accounts, these have become matters for boasting.

I read an article recently about a questionnaire which had been distributed to a large number of people of varying Christian religious denominations, as well as to Jews and agnostics. There was a list of qualities such as Honesty, Ambition, Imagination, Love of Peace, and so on—about eighteen in all, I believe. Each recipient was asked to place these in their order of importance for human life, according to his belief. The results were then classified under the heading of the denomination. There were considerable variations in the rating of every quality with one exception: In every single case Honesty was in the first place. It would seem that no matter how blind men may be to the true nature of honesty, serious human

Fig. 15: The thieves

Fig. 16: The false counselors

beings of good will, be they Catholic, Puritan, Jew, or agnostic, are convinced that honesty is the first essential of the good life. It is not surprising that Dante has put the dishonest and the betrayers in the lowest pit of all.

It is, then, of the highest importance that we look very deeply into the dishonesties to which we unconsciously, or, more often, half-consciously consent. This is no superficial matter of never telling lies; it may be that a lie told on one level is the only way to be loyal to a deeper truth. The crucial question is *why* a man speaks or acts a lie—for personal profit or protection or out of the springs of love—a thing most hard to discriminate. A basic truth of purpose is essential, without which any attempt to confront the unconscious or enter upon the way of individuation is doomed to failure. If we uncover in ourselves the tendency to allow any other value, even the most seemingly noble, to divert us from the necessities of this quest, then we may know that there is somewhere or other an element of fraud in our search. We are usurers, sitting at the rim of that last pit where Satan himself, as we shall see, will either devour us or become the ladder to the stars.

Dante has looked upon Geryon and learned in the bowges the hidden workings of fraud, but on the threshold of the Well he is himself caught for a moment by a falsity of feeling. He listens to the wrangling of two of the falsifiers and begins to enjoy it.

> I was all agog and listening eagerly,
> When the master said: "Yes, feast thine eyes; go on;
> A little more, and I shall quarrel with thee."
>
> (XXX, 130–132)

Dante immediately reacts with another emotional falsity—he shows an altogether disproportionate shame. Virgil rebukes him for this also.

> "Think no more of it; but another time,
>
> Imagine I'm still standing at thy side
> Whenever Fortune, in thy wayfaring,
> Brings thee where people wrangle thus and chide;
>
> It's vulgar to enjoy that kind of thing."
>
> (XXX, 144–148)

It is an exposure of a particular personal weakness; but here on the threshold of the last pit of Hell it is, I think, also a reminder of the danger of looking upon evil, of its power to drag us away from consciousness into identification with itself, through some seemingly small "vulgarity." Dante is awakened to it by Virgil's objectivity, and his words speak to us all of the importance of turning quickly to such imaginative objectivity as we can muster when this kind of shadow reaction threatens us. "Imagine I'm still standing at thy side." Also, I believe, there is great significance in the introduction of this small, mean thing at so late a point of the journey down. "Do not imagine," it says to us, "that your growth in discrimination, your increase of consciousness, means that you are safe from such despicable emotions." The greater the degree of awareness, the more damaging are the vulgarities which in the past were hardly noticeable. If one has awakened, however, remorse is foolish.

Dante now sees in the distance enormous figures whom he

mistakes for towers. They are in fact the giants who stand in a circle round the well of the eighth circle, their feet at the bottom, their huge torsos towering above the rim. By them only may one descend among the betrayers. Dorothy Sayers says of them that they may be taken "as the images of the blind forces which remain in the soul, and in society, when the 'general bond of love' is dissolved and the 'good of the intellect' is wholly withdrawn, and when nothing remains but blocks of primitive mass-emotion. . . ."[4]

> For where the instrument of thinking mind
> Is joined to strength and malice, man's defence
> Cannot avail to meet these powers combined.
>
>   (XXXI, 55–57)

These words need no interpretation in a century which has seen Hitler's Germany and Stalin's Russia, and the many symptoms of just such a horror here and now in our own country among both young and old.

Dante meets three of these most familiar monsters of mass emotion. Nimrod is the first who greets them with a senseless jumble of sounds, words without meaning. He it was who built the tower of Babel, and so he symbolizes the breaking of the clear beauty of constructive imaginative work into empty words that have lost their power to communicate. Virgil says,

Fig. 17: The giants; descent to Cocytus

"We'll waste no words, but leave him where he stands,
For all speech is to him as is to all
That jargon of his which no one understands."

(XXXI, 79–81)

It is not easy in these days to pass by the jargon that besets us and "waste no words." Incidentally, John Ciardi, writing before the 1968 presidential election, said that we should not again have a great president until we elected one who, like all who had been great in the past, could speak that clear and beautiful English without cliches, whereby alone a president may truly interpret their own meaning to the people. Jargon, whether of the intellectual or hippy variety, is born of primitive mass thinking and never of the true feeling-intellect. When we hear it, we may be sure of the emptiness it covers. Nimrod looms dark and menacing in our world.

The second giant is Ephialtes, the image of senseless violence. He is bound by great chains here in the eternal pit, the left hand chained in front, the right behind. Mass violence is in fact a selfbound thing. The giant rages in mindless fury and terrifies Dante, but he is bound; mass violence cannot in fact ever damage or touch the essential integrity of the individual human soul who is, without fraud, upon the way.

The poets now approach Antaeus, who is a very vain giant; and it is he who lifts them down to the bottom of the well when Virgil applies a little guileful flattery and promises that Dante will write about his fame when he returns to earth. Perhaps it is not too fanciful to say that we never really get to the bottom and so start up again unless we press into our service, so to speak, our own personal vanities. How often do we find energy to work on our problems because we can't bear to appear lazy or indifferent in the eyes of our friends, of our guides, of ourselves! Provided always that we are *conscious* of this motive, it can be a powerful help along the way. Antaeus can lift us over an otherwise insuperable barrier. On that other descent into the hell of complete meaninglessness, the mass emotions, the giants, do indeed precipitate mankind into ultimate betrayal. Sayers writes, ". . . one may call them the doom of nonsense, violence, and triviality, overtaking a civilization in which the whole natural order is abrogated."[5] So we arrive among the traitors.

The Exit

"BENEATH THE CLAMOUR, beneath the monotonous circlings, beneath the fires of Hell, here at the centre of the lost soul and the lost city, lie the silence and the rigidity and the eternal frozen cold. It is perhaps the greatest image in the whole *Inferno*. . . . A cold and cruel egotism, gradually striking inward till even the lingering passions of hatred and destruction are frozen into immobility—that is the final state of sin. The conception is, I think, Dante's own. . . . "[6] So Dorothy Sayers writes of the last and ninth circle, the frozen lake of Cocytus.

Here in the bitter cold the poets meet the various types of traitors, betrayers of kindred, country, and guests. These are plunged in the ice up to their necks, held in the paralyzing cold which they have willed by their denial of all the values of human exchange. Among them there is one shade whom Dante recognizes as being a man still alive. The body, says Virgil, can live on though the soul is so dead to all humanity as to lie already in the ice of Hell. Last they see those traitors to their lords who, having deliberately sworn solemn oaths and openly pledged their faith, have broken that faith; even their heads are covered; they are utterly isolated from all contact with anything other than their own egos. This place is called Judecca after Judas, type of that conscious betrayal of God and man which is the final negation of love.

We look now with Dante upon Satan himself.

> Ask me not, Reader; I shall not waste breath
> Telling what words are powerless to express;
>
> This was not life, and yet it was not death. . . .
>
> (XXXIV, 23–25)

He had three faces, one red, one yellow, one black, and six great bat-like wings without feathers, whose flapping generated the winds which froze the lake of Cocytus.

Fig. 18: The traitors

> . . . And he wept
> From his six eyes, and down his triple chin
> Runnels of tears and bloody slaver dripped.

(XXXIV, 52–56)

And with his own claws he flayed his own hide.

The sinners whom he ceaselessly chewed in his mouths were Judas, Brutus, and Cassius. Dorothy Sayers points out that in order to understand this we must get rid of political thinking. Brutus and Cassius here are not simply leaders of rebellion against a system of government they believed corrupt. They are traitors to the Empire, which for Dante meant world-order. They are, therefore, types of the betrayal of all outer fellowship and community, as Judas represents betrayal of inner meaning and of the very roots of love. They are, however, symbols as well as allegories; and their meaning shines out anew in every age for those individuals who make imaginative contact with them.

This particular choice of images for the cannibalism of ultimate evil is another instance of Dante's extraordinary genius for conveying even in his most universal statements an immediately personal and individual meaning. For Judas and Brutus were not only sworn servants of the one they murdered; they were also much-loved friends. It is this that distinguishes them from the other traitors to their lords, and from the betrayers of kindred, country, and guests; it is this that makes them such intensely living symbols of the root of evil.

To betray those bound to us by an involuntary blood tie; to be a traitor to the country we have not chosen but which has nourished and protected us; to deceive the guest whom we have received into our house, offering temporary sanctuary; even the betrayal of a sworn devotion, all these things are an outrage upon human love and decency. But the betrayal of a friend is the final extinction because the love given in true friendship is far more than an instinctive tie or a sense of human obligation, far more than duty, or affection or passion. Friendship is a fully conscious relationship, and it is exceedingly difficult to grow into the purity and freedom of this greatest of all human experiences of love. Emerson wrote that no one could be a friend who was not wholly himself: ". . . the least defect of self-possession vitiates, in my judgment, the entire relation. There can never be deep peace between two spirits, never mutual respect, until, in their dialogue, each stands for the whole world. . . . The essence of friendship is entireness, a total magnanimity and trust."

We cannot doubt that the friendship between Jesus and Judas, between Caesar and Brutus, was of this kind, on this level of awareness. The kiss in the Garden of Gethsemane, surely returned by Jesus (as shown in H. Bosch's unforgettable picture), and Caesar's words as the knife went home, "And thou, my child" (better known through Shakespeare as "et tu, Brute"), convey with piercing beauty the unbreakable nature of a friend's love once and forever given with "total magnanimity and trust," even when this love is betrayed by the loved one. If one who has glimpsed this mystery of love thereafter betrays it, holding it of less value than expediency, a doctrine, or a principle, however noble, or anything whatever in heaven or on earth, then in fact he betrays the totality itself and accepts in its place his thirty pieces of silver.

Certain modern interpretations of Judas' act seem to me to make much more sense than the superficial view of him as an avaricious man, wanting money. The belief that he was an idealist, seeing the necessity of the Crucifixion intellectually, who fell into the insidious evil of putting what he conceived to be the "good of many" above personal truth and loyalty, strikes to the very heart of the matter, especially in this age of passionate fighting for "causes." Brutus did exactly this, killing Caesar for the good of the state. A small man could never have become the friend of Jesus; but a man capable of the maturity of "total magnanimity and trust" is particularly exposed to this terrible delusion about the nature of love. It is true that all minor goals and desires masquerading as love must be sacrificed to love, but never love itself. In the image of Satan devouring the flesh of Judas and Brutus at the center of Hell, Dante, whether consciously or not, has thrust before our eyes with staggering force the truth that Satan, Evil itself, is fed and kept alive by the betrayal of conscious personal love between single individuals. The final treachery to God and the Universe is the setting up of a principle as of more moment than mature love.

It is only when we become fully aware of the nature of this root of all the potential evil within us that we find ourselves climbing, by means of this same realization, up toward the light of truth. Dante, however, is carried at this crucial turning point by his friend and guide, as we too must be carried at such a time when we look upon the horror of the traitor within. Like Dante, we must trust "as a little child" to the inner guide if we are to awaken to the truth that the way down is the way up. Virgil says,

> ". . . we have seen all."

> Then, as he bade, about his neck I curled
> My arms and clasped him. And he spied the time
> And place; and when the wings were wide unfurled
>
> Set him upon the shaggy flanks to climb,
> And thus from shag to shag descended down
> 'Twixt matted hair and crusts of frozen rime.
>
> And when we had come to where the huge thigh-bone
> Rides in its socket at the haunch's swell,
> My guide, with labour and great exertion,
>
> Turned head to where his feet had been, and fell
> To hoisting himself up upon the hair,
> So that I thought us mounting back to Hell.
>> (XXXIV, 69–81)

Virgil, urging Dante to hold fast, for there is no other way out of such evil, emerges at last, panting and tired, "through a rocky vent" and puts his burden down. To his amazement, Dante sees Satan's hairy legs sticking up above his head. Once past the generative organs of evil the down becomes up and up becomes down. The poets are climbing towards the antipodes. (They have passed the center of the earth and gravity is reversed.)

Fig. 19: Emergence from Hell

Up a small steep path, beside the descending stream of Lethe, the poets climb now without rest.

> He first, I following; till my straining sense
> Glimpsed the bright burden of the heavenly cars
> Through a round hole; by this we climbed, and thence
>
>   Came forth, to look once more upon the stars.
>   (XXXIV, 136–139)

It is rebirth, and it is Easter morning.

The Purgatorio

The Threshold of the Mountain

A. THE NEW ATTITUDE

IT IS NEAR DAWN as Dante climbs out of the narrow opening and looks upon the stars. Behind him is the darkness of the pit, monotonous, dirty, a blackness of meaningless confusion and clamor; before him is the clean, sapphire-blue darkness out of which the great stars shine—Venus, the planet of Love, and the four brilliant stars of the southern pole to which fallen man is blind. It is thought possible that Dante had heard of the Southern Cross; but, whether he had or not, the symbol of the fourfold nature of reality springs from his unconscious, shining upon the threshold of the great climb to the Earthly Paradise where man regains his innocence.

The effect upon us of this image is far more powerful than if the poets emerged from the dark pit into clear sunlight, for implicit in it is the whole meaning of this crucial transition-point in the life of a man or woman. We do not suddenly exchange our thralldom to the unconscious fogs and the sufferings of neurosis for a wholly conscious and sunlit climb to the heights. What we do experience at this moment is a total transformation of the nature of the darkness itself—or rather of our attitude towards it. As long as we seek to escape from our various "hells" into freedom from pain, we remain irremediably bound; we can emerge from the pains of Hell in one way only—by accepting another kind of suffering, the suffering which is purging, instead of meaningless damnation. The souls in the *Purgatorio* suffer the same kind of torments as those in the *Inferno*; but they suffer with willing acceptance instead of with bitter resentment, because they have dared to recognize meaning and to accept responsibility. They have glimpsed from afar the planet Venus, the true nature of Love, and deep in their hearts is born the vision of the four stars of the pole, the pattern of wholeness. Thus the moment when a man steps over the threshold onto the shore of Purgatory is the moment in which he is ready in the core of his being to follow *at any cost* the way to the realization of this vision in his own individual life. It is a way which will inevitably lead him through the agony whereby the "I want, I must have" of the ego is transmuted into the Love whose "center is everywhere."

In the lifetime of every man there surely comes, at the deepest level, such a moment of choice, whether fully recognized or not. Sometimes it comes very early, sometimes not until the moment of physical death. Yet as T.S. Eliot says, "the time of death is every moment," and so therefore is the time of choice. However, even when the basic choice of direction has been truly made, nevertheless in our weakness we are continually falling back into the neurotic, ego-centered torments of Hell, and so the new attitude must be constantly reaffirmed. Almost daily this great image of Dante's passage from the blind murk to the shining dark may come to our aid. We have but to turn ourselves upside down, reverse our attitude, for Satan's legs, the evil itself, to become the ladder to the narrow opening; for the misery and shame that engulf us to become the very way to the vision of the stars. We fail, however, and lose heart, because we so quickly forget that this change is impossible without a total willingness to "pay the uttermost farthing"—if necessary over a long period of time. Instead we expect to be transported immediately into an infantile paradise, as Dante did in the dark wood. Purgatory is not an outmoded doctrine invented by the Roman Catholic Church; it is an immediate reality in the life of every man and woman who chooses the way of individuation.

B. The New Atmosphere

Anyone who has experienced this emergence from an attitude of remorse and resentment to an attitude of repentance and acceptance knows the extraordinary sense of a total change of atmosphere that goes with it. In place of a grey monotony and heaviness, everything and everyone around us is bathed in freshness and filled with meaning. From the first words of the *Purgatorio*, through all the descriptions of suffering, until we reach the joy of the Forest at the summit, Dante evokes with extraordinary vividness the clean and sparkling *delight* of the atmosphere. We are pierced through and through with wonder at this sense of clarity; and, by the mere reading of such "angelic verse," feel cleansed and purged ourselves. "Within the all-pervading atmosphere of 'delight renewed' the change of outlook defines itself with endless subtlety. Courtesy is everywhere the key-note."[7]

There is a clear distinction between this atmosphere of delight in the midst of pain and the unclouded joy of the blessed in the *Paradiso*, for which the mountain is the training ground. As far as words can define the difference, "delight" and "joy" must serve. On the first page of the *Purgatorio*, Dante writes:

> For to the second realm I tune my tale,
> Where human spirits purge themselves, and train
> To leap up into joy celestial.
>
>   (I, 4–6)

He continues, though the sun has not yet risen:

> Colour unclouded . . .
>
> Brought to mine eyes renewal of delight
> So soon as I came forth from that dead air
> Which had oppressed my bosom and my sight.
>
>   (I, 13–18)

I shall now quote at some length from Dorothy Sayers' very beautiful and sensitive description of the mountain so that we may feel its atmosphere around us as we travel with Dante from terrace to terrace.

> Hell is black, confined, stinking, noisy, and suffocating. The great Mountain of Purgatory rises in a pure sunlit solitude out of the windswept southern sea where never man set sail; nothing disturbs its calm, and the silence of its lofty spaces is scarcely broken save by the murmur of prayer and the crying of angelic voices; only when a soul is released to its triumph does the whole Mount quake and thunder with the shout of jubilee. And by night and day the flaming hosts of Heaven, which never were seen in Hell—the undimmed sun, the moon like a burnished mazer, the starry habitations of the Zodiac—wheel round the alien pole through a sky that knows no clouds. The whole landscape is washed in with a sweet and delicate austerity. At the Mountain's base, reeds and sand; the

illimitable ocean in the dawnlight; the changing of the sky from orient sapphire through rose and gold to blue; the tang of the clean sea-breezes. On the lower slopes, which lie within earth's atmosphere, grass, with great ridges and outcrops of rock, and, nestling between two spurs of the Mountain, the secluded . . . Valley of the Rulers, suddenly touched in with strong and vivid colour. . . . But once past Peter's Gate and beyond the sphere of air, the hues of living nature vanish. . . . the Mountain is naked rock to the summit; . . . "He brought me out of the horrible pit, out of the mire and clay, and set my feet upon the rock and ordered my goings."

And there, at length—when we have passed through the fire of the last cornice . . . —there is the Forest.[8]

There are no dreams in Hell; there are no dreams in Heaven; for both realms are outside time. When we are possessed by the archetypes in the unconscious we cannot relate to them, and there is no process, no dialogue between dream and consciousness; the dream world has swallowed us up, and we are driven round and round forever at the mercy of instinctive drives and ego-desires. At the other end of the scale, when we shall have come to the state of bliss, these same archetypes will be known as the great angelic and human powers of the psyche, their ambivalence transcended as they revolve around the center. Again this state is beyond time and the opposites, and each individual will have found his place in the eternal dance.

Purgatory, however, is the way between these two states, and is symbolic of the work we do in the dimension of time—the day by day suffering of the tension between the opposites and the long battle for consciousness. On the mountain, therefore, there is the alternation of day and night and a very urgent sense of time.

The souls are unwilling to waste one moment of the daylight in spite of their great pleasure in talking to Dante. It is a point which awakens us to a truth so easily forgotten in this age—the truth that the way of individuation demands *attention*, not just for a few hours or weeks, or a few minutes a day, but, ultimately, during every moment of our lives. I am reminded of the Zen master who was so disconcerted when he realized he had put his umbrella down without noticing the exact place.

How he would have approved of Dante's extreme precision in his descriptions of the images of bliss! The experience of immortality will spring ultimately from constant attention to the "minute particular," in Blake's phrase. The point lies not in *what* we do, as the Puritans mistakenly defined this truth, but in the degree of our conscious awareness of every act and every impulse in their contexts outer and inner. True spontaneity is born of this awareness alone.

In the daytime, then, in the *Purgatorio*, when the sun is shining, we feel the necessity of unremitting effort. But there is another law of the mountain; during the night it is impossible for anyone to take one step upward. The traveler must be still and wait, unless he chooses to walk down the mountain again. Theologically this is interpreted to mean that when the light of grace, the Sun, is withdrawn, the pilgrim falls into a spiritual dryness and aridity during which time he must simply wait in faith for the sun to rise again and resist the temptation to fall back. True indeed; but there is another depth of meaning—particularly for us in this century, individually and collectively, caught as we are in the tremendous overemphasis placed by our society on activity, intellectual, physical, or emotional. In the few words which define this law of the mountain, it is made abundantly clear that if we do not spend the nights—that is, half of our time—being still, we shall effectually extinguish the possibility of growth and walk backwards. In other words, if we do not give validity to the dark, the Yin, the feminine and the receptive; if we do not consent to do nothing, to allow time for dreaming, for listening to the voice of the unconscious, then we shall be in far worse case than if we waste time during the "day," for our excessive activity will lead us backwards, and all will be to do again. On each of the three nights that Dante spent in Purgatory he dreamed. We cannot climb the mountain at all without the cooperation of the unconscious.

It seems to me that the symbol of the Divine Grace without which all our activity is of little avail comes as powerfully to us nowadays through Dante's dreams as through the image of the daytime sun. We shall look at these dreams in detail as we proceed up the mountain; it is enough here to say that each of them represents a leap in Dante's individual awareness—wisdom from the unconscious given and heard in the passivity of the dark, nourishing the hard conscious work of the day and being nourished by it. Dreams, the images which spring out of the dark, are the free gift of Grace, falling on us like dew from Heaven, bringing freshness and strength for our striving under the Sun.

C. The New Penalties

As Dante and Virgil stand on the shore of the mountain and look upon the stars, it is well to reflect upon the nature of the torments they have left behind in the Pit and of those they are about to see as they climb.

There are no punishments in the *Inferno* or in the *Purgatorio*. Punishment is something imposed from without, and the popular idea of sinners punished by a condemning Deity is totally alien to Dante's vision. The word "penalty," however, means the payment of a debt; every act or attitude, insofar as it does not spring from the wholeness beyond the opposites, carries within itself its own penalty. This truth is defined by the East in the doctrine of Karma and by Dante through the extraordinary fitness of his images of suffering. The souls, whether in Hell or Purgatory, are tormented either by the true nature of the sin itself or by its opposite, which is the same thing in reverse.

If we compare the condition of Paolo and Francesca in the second circle of Hell with the suffering of the lustful on the seventh cornice of Purgatory, we see very clearly how the torment in both states springs from the nature of lust itself. In Purgatory the redeemed souls walk in the fierce heat of the fire, whereas there the lovers were mercilessly blown by the cold wind. Desire is hot, but lust which remains unconscious is ultimately cold. The fire of Purgatory is not a condemnation of desire; Dante knows that there is no redemption through cold repression. On the contrary it symbolizes the free acceptance of the terrible burning of the desire itself endured with full realization of its redemptive meaning; so, passing through the fire, the soul finds love.

To take one more example: the Wrathful in Hell lie choking and spluttering in sticky black mud; the Wrathful in Purgatory are blinded by a thick and gritty smoke. We might expect punishment by fire for anger, but anger is never a bringer of light and warmth; on the contrary it is essentially a cold and blinding thing, stifling all discrimination and warmth of heart, so that we cannot see things and people as they are, nor can we ourselves be seen. Dante says of the sullen wrathful in Hell that their "hearts smouldered with a sulky smoke." The difference between the sufferers in Hell and those in Purgatory is again only in their attitude. The angry shades in the mud of the Styx shout curses. Marco Lombardo in the *Purgatorio* says, ". . . though the smoke has made us blind, hearing instead of sight shall neighbour us."

"Hearing instead of sight shall neighbour us." The literal translation is "Hearing shall keep us joined." These words, coming to us with such gracious courtesy out of the smoke, express a fundamental attitude of all the souls in the *Purgatorio*, an attitude of enormous importance to each one of us. Even after the fundamental consent to pay the price has been given, how easy it is to say, "I am in a fog—in the grip of my shadow side, and I have to get rid of this or that weakness *before* I can be free enough to attend to other people or embark on some positive relationship; I am not yet ready." And so, forgetting that if we cannot see, we can hear, or if we cannot hear we can see, we become obsessed with the smoke, or with whatever other form of tension and suffering the shadow creates for us; and pretty soon we are back in the infernal dark. The souls on Dante's mountain, while they never allow themselves to be distracted from the pain and tension which awareness of the shadow brings, yet give to the travelers as they pass their full attention, with such of their faculties as *are* free to hear, to see, or to speak. There is no slightest hint of that deadly attitude: "I am no good because of this or that or the other weakness, and you can't possibly want to associate with me"; nor of its opposite: "Stay with me, distract me, pull me out of this awful pain." The purging process is immediately halted when we lose that objective courtesy to others, to ourselves, to life in all its manifestations, which is conveyed in those words, "though the smoke has made us blind, hearing instead of sight shall neighbour us."

CHAPTER 7

The Shore

THE POETS HAVE quite a long way to go before they pass the next gateway and enter Purgatory proper. "Peter's Gate" is not reached until they have climbed almost a third of the way up the mountain and have passed through the region which Dante calls Ante-Purgatory.

We left them standing beside the dark hole from which they have emerged; but before he can start at all on the new journey, Dante must pass a kind of entrance examination. He is confronted by Cato, the guardian of the threshold, who questions him somewhat roughly. Virgil answers and explains the situation with great respect, flattering Cato a little, for which the latter brusquely rebukes him. Cato stands for the strict moral virtues of the Stoic. He is the only person on the mountain who speaks ungraciously, a hint that the Stoic virtues know nothing of Grace, from which springs courtesy in action; and it is probable that Dante makes him the guardian of the approach to Purgatory in order to stress that in the ecstasy of that first vision of the stars lies a danger—the temptation to forget the necessity for discipline. The dour figure of Cato barring the way to the heights of being carries an apt warning for us nowadays, when such things as drug-induced or even meditation-induced visions lure men all too easily into the delusion that such ecstasies are ends in themselves, unrelated to life and behavior in this world. While moral disciplines alone cannot ever rise beyond the shore of the mountain, as Cato could not, nevertheless without them we cannot take one step on the way to individuation. Only after the long climb is a man free from all law—free to love and do as he wills.

Two things, says Cato, must be done before the journey may be continued. Virgil must wash Dante's face and clean off the filth of Hell, and he must gird his pupil's waist with one of the reeds which grow in the water on the shore—reeds which can withstand wind and wave because they bend before

Fig. 20: The arrival in Ante-Purgatory; Cato

the storm. Those who seem to regard being dirty as some sort of proof that they are free of all foolish conformity would do well to hear the message of Cato. The failure to wash his face may well be a sign that a man is in some way or another cut off from the real values of the "dirt," the soil.

The other imperative is that the ego must be girded with humility, without which all experience of the numinous must lead ultimately to the fate of Icarus. The rope girdle of "good resolutions," which Dante had to abandon in the pit, is now replaced by the girdle of the humble reed. How moving is the pattern of these images! Dante had to go down into the pit of fraud and look upon the ultimate darkness without any support from his hitherto noble intentions. Only when he has emerged from this black experience is he ready and able to know the humility without which all our visions of light lead only to an inflation of the ego. When we are girdled with the reed we are safe, however high we mount, encircled by that which grows only from the waters in the low places of the earth.

Moreover the sound of the reeds, the whisper of the wind blowing through them, often symbolizes in myth and fairy tale the voice of the inner wisdom. They whisper to the hero or heroine (as in the Eros and Psyche story) the solution to the impossible task, and no man can take a step up the Mountain until he is quiet enough to hear and humble enough to listen to their message.

We may fitly pause here on the shore beside the reeds to say a word about the symbolism of mountains. Since the middle ages we have climbed so high on the skyscrapers of the intellect that the image of climbing anything is apt to strike us as negative. We are desperately aware of our need to go down, to find truth and wisdom which has sunk into the unconscious, having realized that our upward strivings lead only to false spirituality or empty theory. Nevertheless the climb is still an essential of the way; and the effort and hardship involved in mountain climbing speak as powerfully as ever to the imagination, especially when we think of this climb in contrast to the elevators which we construct to shoot us up to the top of the lofty buildings of our split thinking.

"Often the mountain," says Dr. Marie Louise von Franz in one of her lectures on fairy tales, "is the goal of a long quest or the site of the transition into eternity. The mountain also marks the place—the point in life—where the hero, after arduous effort (climbing) becomes oriented and gains steadfastness and self knowledge, values that develop through the effort to become conscious in the process of individuation."[9] The Mountain of Purgatory is precisely such a place, as we shall see.

In the *I Ching* there is a sign called Humility or Modesty; in our context we could call it the sign of the Reed. The image for this sign is the Mountain *within* the Earth. This is surely the point of the reed girdle; we must stay, as it were, within the earth as we climb the mountain to reach "the site of the transition into eternity."

The sun rises as the poets stand on the shore, uncertain of their way. Dante sees a white light moving swiftly towards them over the sea, which he presently makes out to be great white wings on the prow of a boat. It is the ship of souls with its angel pilot.

This is the first of the angels whom we meet in the *Purgatorio*, and in the few lines of his breathtaking description, Dante sweeps away once and for all any images we may retain of gentle beings floating about in a vaguely comforting way; instead we are suddenly confronted with a power of the spirit beyond our knowing. We are forced to our knees in awe as was Dante himself, by the sheer beauty of the image; and then for an instant perhaps we may feel within ourselves a touch

of the towering strength, the grace and swiftness, the inde-
scribable otherness of angelic reality. Virgil speaks:

> "Down, down!" he cried, "fold hands and bow thy knees;
> Behold the angel of the Lord! Henceforth
> Thou shalt see many of these great emissaries.
>
> See how he scorns all instruments of earth,
> Needing no oar, no sail but his own wings,
> 'Twixt shores that span so vast an ocean's girth.
>
> See how each soaring pinion heavenward springs,
> Beating the air with pens imperishable
> That are not mewed like mortal coverings."
>
> And near and nearer as he came full sail
> The bird of God shone momently more bright,
> So that mine eyes endured him not, but fell.
> . . . .
>
> Freehold of bliss apparent in his face,
> The heavenly pilot on the poop stood tiptoe
> And with him full an hundred souls had place.
>
> "*In exitu Israel de Aegypto*,"
> From end to end they sang their holy lay
> In unison; and so he brought the ship to.
>
>   (II, 28–48)

Fig. 21: The angel pilot; Casella

My first reading of the *Commedia* was not much short of half a century ago, and I had the good fortune to be introduced to it by Professor Cesare Foligno, great scholar and lover of Dante, who held the chair of Italian at Oxford in the 1920s. There are certain incidents in the poem that have remained with me through all the years, so vividly imprinted on my imagination that I can still hear his rich voice speaking the lines. This passage is one of them.

The mind flies back to the souls crossing Acheron into Hell, cursing, pushing, beaten by Charon's oar, all fellowship rejected; and against this background the image of the ship of singing souls shines with an even greater radiance. "When Israel came out of Egypt"—they sing in unison; the gateway to Purgatory is release from the bondage, release from the neurotic suffering, into the clean air of a long purging in the wilderness; the journey into joy has begun.

CHAPTER 8

The Place of Waiting

THE FIRST TWO terraces of the mountain leading up to Peter's Gate are called by Dante Ante-Purgatory. They are places of waiting. Dorothy Sayers says that only here are the punishments imposed from without. I do not agree that this is so; for although the time of waiting is a prescribed number of years for each group, this seems to spring as logically from the nature of the sin as any of the other penalties. The souls on these terraces are people who have for one reason or another continually put off the moment of decisive consent to the discipline of *time*. They are those who have been unable to put a term to old ways and attitudes long after the capacity is there, or people who for one reason or another have never accepted the limitations of time nor been really aware of its reality. We know well the continual cry, "I have no time!" which betrays this blindness. We do not *possess* time. We do not know what it is, but it gives form and order to the universe; and unless we relate to it consciously our lives will "dissolve in the boundless," as the *I Ching* says. If we try to *have* time, time possesses us and we are continually driven by it, which means that we have never fully consented to life on this earth. "Only through time, time is conquered," T.S. Eliot wrote in *The Four Quartets*. The "hours" of the monastic day and the austere discipline of time have been the bedrock of the formal religious life through which many men have in all ages sought consciousness of eternity. Today this outer form is for very few, but the truth it embodies must be found by every individual who seeks the wholeness which is both beyond time and includes it.

The souls in Ante-Purgatory, therefore, must experience the inevitability of the nature of time. The term of years during which they must remain there is set and unalterable, just as the rhythms of nature are unalterable. Nine months, for instance, must pass between the conception and birth of a child, and there is nothing we can do about it. We do not say that this is imposed from without, but that it is an intrinsic "law of nature"; and so those (most of us) who have lived in a continual state of hurry or delay are purged here before the gate of Purgatory by the necessity to accept a time of waiting, as intrinsic to the psyche as nature's laws are to her rhythms of growth.

There is, however, one way in which this time of waiting may be shortened. All the souls in Ante-Purgatory show a great eagerness to ask Dante for his prayers when he returns to earth, for only through the prayers of the living may they come more quickly to Peter's Gate. In Purgatory proper, also, the intercession of another can shorten the time of a man's suffering on the mountain, although he can never actually be *relieved* of this kind of pain; indeed it is the last thing the soul in Purgatory would ask to be relieved of. Belaqua in Ante-Purgatory, on the terrace of the pre-occupied, tells Dante that he longs for prayers in order to hasten his entry *into* the healing pain of Purgatory—the pain of self-knowledge. "Prayer from a heart in grace," he says, "for who sets store by other kinds, which are not heard above?"

From these images we may draw a deep insight into the nature of intercession, of human "exchange" in the inner world. "A heart in grace"—that is, in contact with the Self, with the *whole* reality, is heard above, and no other. In our language this means that only such a heart can be a channel of real healing to another, for it is heard above; that is, it awakens others from the fogs of their partial aims to a higher consciousness, to a deeper awareness of, and devotion to, the mystery within. These things are *caught* through the unconscious from others. We all know that without our contacts with those whose inner certainty and mature love flows out from them to each unique person, our own journey towards freedom would be immeasurably lengthened; indeed it would never have begun. There is an Indian text in which it is said that these contacts are the *only* way to reality. The intercession, the selfless offer of love and compassion from another, is the prayer which can save us from neurotic and pointless suffering and awaken us to the pain of the mountain; it can even hasten our release from this pain also, when we have grown into full acceptance of it and are able in our turn to offer such a love to another. This is what Beatrice did for Dante and perhaps—who knows?—also what he did for her.

All of us, whether we will or no, are constantly putting out "prayers" through the unconscious into the environment, for all intensely concentrated desire is a kind of prayer; and it enters into the unconscious of others, affecting them to a greater or lesser degree, giving strength or stealing it away. It behooves us then to realize our great responsibility. Only to the degree that our desire is free of demand for anything at all, even for what we conceive to be good, is prayer valid. Without the passionate desire to relieve others of pain and misery we would be inhuman monsters, but this desire only becomes prayer heard above when we endure its burning and pass beyond it to the death of our own demands (not our desires) to be freed from suffering. Then, and only then, will our action for others in the outer world spring from the pattern of our own lives as they touch others, and not from anxious or complacent busyness. The man whose heart is "in grace" can carry another's burden because he consciously bears his own. He can then enter with deep imaginative compassion into the suffering of others, and by this, his prayer, the burdens of self-pity and tortured conflict are lifted from us, our inner gaze is drawn with his to the Center, and we are carried swiftly forward on the mountain way.

It has been truly said that all prayer is answered, or in other words, that the thing we basically and for the most part unconsciously desire with great intensity, we always receive. This is implicit in Dante's doctrine that Hell is desired by the damned or they would not be there. We rarely recognize the answers to our hidden prayers since we don't know what they are. A parent, for example, who, while genuinely convinced he or she wants only the best for a child, may actually be possessed by an implacable desire for the child to fulfill some unlived aspect of his own life. He may pray daily for God's blessing on the child, but this cannot possibly be "heard above" since the real prayer in his heart is the desire to impose his own image on the child and to take away his freedom; and the prayer is certainly answered, seeping as it does from birth into the unconscious of the child, whether he tries to live up to the image or rebels violently against it. Through struggle and suffering, as he grows, he may free his personality from the parent's prayer, but there are many whose lives may remain distorted.

This is simply one obvious example of the kind of hidden desires, masquerading as love, which spring from all our evasions, all our refusals to know what we are really asking for. They are the prayers of a heart *not* "in grace"; and though they are not "heard above," as Belaqua puts it, that is, they do not increase consciousness, they are most certainly heard below in the unconscious; and the one "prayed for" may be dragged away from the freedom of his true identity, his unique pattern.

For an example of the highest level of the prayer of a heart in grace we may remember the moving account of Julia de Beausobre in the OGPU prison.[10] She found the strength to maintain her identity in the face of prolonged mental torture, because she knew that her refusal to betray her friends and, with them, her own integrity, was the only prayer she could offer for the torturers themselves in their terrible degradation. So too, the Rainmaker in the Chinese story, when asked to pray for rain, sought only to confront the darkness in himself, invaded as he was by the collective atmosphere of fear and misery, and to make contact again with his true identity "above," beyond anxiety and conflict. Thus, through his prayer that asked for nothing, came the blessing of rain on the whole land. This is the true prayer of intercession, described by Dante as love fulfilling in "one fire's flash" the debt of another.

In all the great religions of the world, the saints, sages, and gurus have been known as the "intercessors" for humanity, the links between God and man. They are those who have "yielded themselves between," in the root meaning of the verb, "to intercede." *Cedere* means to walk, to yield, and, in some contexts, to die or to be transformed. All these meanings are relevant to those who truly intercede. They stand in the gap between darkness and light, pain and joy, evil and good, and transcend them all because their personal desires have all burned away in the fire of their love and compassion. Who knows how much every man owes to them? For these great ones accept and confront the darkness consciously, so drawing off the shadow from others. In our century Carl Jung, among so many others, mostly unknown, has made this confrontation and draws our eyes with his to the peace beyond.

This, then, is the prayer of the heart in grace, into which we too can daily enter to the extent to which we are able to open ourselves to darkness, and letting go of each demand for a false peace as it comes to us, carry our own burden to the end.

Before we resume the journey, there is another brief conversation, in this context of prayer, that brings out Dante's genius for lightening and making human his most profound discussions by a sudden warm personal touch. Dante meets and talks with a lady called Pia dei Tolomei. All the other people mentioned in Ante-Purgatory are male; Pia, like them, begs for Dante's prayers, but she adds something that most men would never think of, but which is a natural thought in a true woman. "Pray," she says, "when thou returnest to the world and art well rested from the weary way." This gracious feminine concern for Dante as an ordinary human being who gets tired is sheer delight in the midst of such great matters.

The Excommunicate on the first terrace are those cut off from the Sacraments of the Church who did not make their peace with it until the moment of death. To us they may symbolize people caught in the wrong kind of individualism—those who will not listen in humility to any traditional wisdom or to anyone else's experience or accept any authority, and so reject the truth of fellowship here on this earth, because they imagine this is the way to become a free person. There is plenty of that in our world, and such an attitude precludes the sacramental or symbolic life which is the meeting point of eternity with time.

Those on the second terrace, the indolent, the unshriven, and the preoccupied, are more obviously sinners against time. In the indolent this is plain, and to them may be added their polar opposites, those impatient souls who are in such a hurry to arrive that they try to jump ahead of the ordered passage of the hours. The unshriven are those who have died suddenly by violence or by murder, and the superficial reaction is that these have been the victims of circumstances. But let us remember that assuredly the manner of a man's death is implicit in his life; it has been truly said that there could be no murder without an unconsciously willing murderee. The unshriven are men who were not conscious at the moment of death, and, in our life here, they are the so-called victims of violent solutions to inner as well as outer conflicts; thus, to die unshriven would mean the refusal to accept any change involving a death of ego-demands. We often see this in dreams. We are shown that it is time for a death; and we have the choice either to accept this through a conscious sacrifice or to allow a violent death in the unconscious whereby we are doomed, perhaps, to many years of waiting before the opportunity for transformation comes again.

The last of these groups in Ante-Purgatory, however, is the

Fig. 22: The indolent

one perhaps nearest to our daily experience—the group of the preoccupied or "do-gooders." In the Valley of the Rulers we meet them—the good kings and potentates who never had time to attend to their own interior life because they were so busy and troubled about many things and people. As Dorothy Sayers remarks, there need be no doubt that Dante would include amongst the preoccupied such people as "anxious parents, over-burdened housewives and breadwinners, social workers, busy organizers, and others who are so 'rushed off their feet' that they forget to say their prayers."[11] We might add many more, such as those overworked doctors, psychologists, priests, and ministers who never have a moment for real introversion; indeed all those who take refuge from themselves in an unreflective pursuit of good, pouring all their energy into the redemption of society or the succor of other people, while blind to their personal darkness.

These people live out their time of waiting in a place of great

THE PURGATORIO

beauty; for, after all, they have been busy in the service of something other than themselves; their concern for other people has been truly sincere. The Valley of the Rulers sparkles with jewel-like colors.

> Gold and fine silver, crimson and ceruse,
> Wood yellow-lustrous, clear cerulean dye,
> Indigo, fresh-cracked emerald's brilliant hues,
>
> Matched with the foliage and the flowers that lie
> Heaped in that lap, would faint, as minor faints
> Beneath its major, and show dim thereby.
>
>   (VII, 73–78)

The description reminds one of certain dreams in which the colors of nature have this kind of vividness beyond the vision of the waking eye.

Into this beautiful valley the poets move as the sun sets and the light fades. They see that the whole host of shades stand watching the sky.

> And then I saw descending from above
> Two angels, bearing fiery swords in hand,
> Broke short and bated at the points thereof.
>
> Green as fresh leaves new-budded on a wand
> Their raiment was, which billowed out and blew
> Behind, by flutter of green pinions fanned.
>
>   (VIII, 25–30)

These angels, or "great emissaries" in Virgil's phrase, come to rest on each side of the valley. Then, while Dante is talking to one of the shades (all of whom, by the way, are still typically fussing about what is going on on the earth), he sees a great snake come into the valley, slithering over the green grass. At once the angels leap into the air on their shining green wings. As they move towards it with their blunt swords, the snake turns and is gone. This, it is explained, happens every evening.

There are certain incidents in the *Commedia* which, I always feel, have a specifically dream-like flavor, and this is one of them. It is the kind of dream which comes to many people in widely differing images, of course, at a certain point of their growth when they have worked hard and long to recognize their inner darkness—have passed through Hell as Dante has—

and have reached a stage where to go on searching out and analyzing every detail of the shadow contents of the unconscious is worse than unnecessary, indeed, definitely regressive. In the *I Ching* there is a line, "Penetration under the bed. . . . Perseverance brings misfortune." There are times when we must simply fix our eyes on the emissary, the angel, the intuition of the Self in the unconscious, and when even he needs no sharp sword. The cold-blooded inhumanity of the snake in this context is harmless under "the swish and swoop of the green wings." It is a time not to fight the shadow but to overgrow it. It seems peculiarly apt that this message comes to the do-gooders; for, when we are prone to be very busy about good works, we find it extremely difficult not to be over-busy about the dark things, trying to banish them, especially from other people's lives. We have indeed to be aware of them, to look at the shadow and to keep still, and then the angels will come without our aid. The angels are green—the color of hope and of the natural *growing* things of the earth, which emerge in their own time.

It is likewise no accident that this vision comes to Dante when the waiting time is over and immediately before he is carried up to the gateway of Purgatory proper. All busyness must now be left behind because the training for contemplative life is about to begin. As he sits in the valley the sun sets, the moon rises, and Dante sleeps and, sleeping, dreams.

> I dreamt I saw an eagle in mid-air,
> Plumed all in gold, hovering on wings outspread,
> As though to make his swoop he poised him there.
>
> Meseemed me in the place whence Ganymede
> Up to the high gods' halls was snatched one day
> Leaving his comrades all discomfited.
>
> I thought: Perhaps this eagle strikes his prey
> Always just here; his proud feet would think shame
> Elsewhere to seize and carry it away.
>
> Then, in my dream, he wheeled awhile and came
> Down like the lightening, terrible and fast,
> And caught me up into the sphere of flame,

Where he and I burned in one furnace-blast;
The visionary fire so seared me through,
It broke my sleep perforce, and the dream passed.

> (IX, 19–33)

He wakes in great fear.

. . . the dream fled and left the face of me
Pale, as of one whom fear congeals like frost.

> (IX, 41–42)

The lines powerfully constellate the opposites—the searing heat of the fire and the pale cold fear—a hint of all the opposites to be transcended on the spiral way of Purgatory and a foretaste in the unconscious of his actual experience of the fire on the last cornice. Once more there are all the marks of an actual dream.

In the myth which is Dante's "association" to the dream, Ganymede, beloved by Zeus, was snatched up by him in the form of an eagle from Mount Ida, where he was hunting with friends, and became the cup-bearer of the gods on Olympus. In this moment, preceding a great breakthrough of new consciousness, the dreamer is also about to become a "cup-bearer" of the god; and this is experienced in dreams today as often as ever, and in similar images; the lightening strikes or we are seized upon as if, indeed, by a bird of prey. The most significant difference between Dante's individual dream and the mythological association lies in the image of the searing fire into which the eagle carries him. To be a cup-bearer of the gods, at this stage of his or our journey, does not mean a peaceful waiting upon the gods beyond the conflicts and tensions of conscious and unconscious; it means, on the contrary, to enter the fire and suffer the purging of these conflicts until out of them is born a love freed from all concupiscence—that which Jung called "the transcendent function."

The image of the cup-bearer is particularly powerful for the Christian, since the cup is a central image of the suffering of Christ. "This cup shall not pass from me, till all be fulfilled." When we take up and carry the cup to the Christ within, we pass once and for all from neurotic to innocent suffering and enter the purgatorial state of consciousness. Associations are many and profound—the Mass, the Grail legend, the ancient mysteries of Egypt and Greece. In all of them the cup contained the mystery of mysteries, the essence of the Godhead. For Dante, then, the carrying of the cup is to be a burning in the "visionary fire," and the ego, as always, is terrified. When he awakes, however, his fear recedes, for Virgil explains to him that during the night he has indeed been carried up and is now at the very gate of Purgatory itself. Santa Lucia, St. Lucy, has come and lifted him sleeping, up the last hard climb and has set him down upon the threshold. Santa Lucia had a special significance for Dante. It was through her that the Virgin Mary sent a message to Beatrice bidding her go to Dante's help in the dark wood. She must have been a much loved image to him. He calls her "Lucy, foe to every cruelty."

"I thought," says Dante, "Perhaps this eagle strikes his prey always just here." We are not seized upon by the eagle plumed all in gold until we have reached this point on the mountain of transition to eternity by our own long effort to face the darkness, so that our attitude has radically changed and we are ready to step over the next threshold into a new phase of growth. The contrast between the fierce eagle in Dante's dream and the gentleness of the lady, whose name is light and who actually lifts him to the gate, is extreme, and at first is puzzling. We must remember that Dante does not himself see

Fig. 23: The eagle and Lucy

St. Lucy—he is merely told about her on waking. As yet he cannot be directly aware of Santa Lucia, the holy light, the feminine wisdom of God; for the meeting with Beatrice is still far ahead; first he must experience that same light of inner wisdom as a fiery furnace into which he is thrust by the eagle—and the eagle for him was the symbol of the justice of God. The fire to him is still justice, not love. At this point, however willing we may try to be, we do not have the courage or strength to enter the fire consciously; but we do know that we have been seized upon by a power that will not let us go. For whatever reason we may have entered upon the journey, there comes to most of us a moment when we know that we are "caught," that never again shall we be free to follow the old unconscious path, however often we faint and fail. If this feeling does not come, then our efforts have little meaning and had better be dropped. We cannot enter Peter's Gate unless we are thus "seized upon."

We may well have such a dream as Dante's at this point, and on waking in great fear, realize dimly as we sense its meaning, through the "Virgil" within us, that the burning and the fear are in their totality a promise of peace, of new light and awareness. Like Dante, we cannot yet encounter these things consciously; nevertheless their presence has carried us imperceptibly to the new threshold. We are, as he was, comforted by this knowledge and eager now to cross onto the spiral way.

> "Fear nothing," said my lord, "sit thou secure
> At heart; we've come into a good estate,
> Faint not, but be the more alert therefore.
>
> Thou hast reached Purgatory; see, the great
> Rampart of rock that compasses it round;
> And where the cleft shows yonder, there's the gate."
>
> (IX, 46–51)

Peter's Gate

THE GATE OF HELL stood wide open; the gate of the City of Dis was guarded by demons whom no human power could conquer; but the gate which is the entrance to Purgatory opens to him who knocks and knows the meaning of his knocking.

An angel is the gate-keeper, holding the keys of Peter, one of gold and one of silver; and before the great bronze door are three steps. The first is of gleaming white marble, so highly polished that it is a mirror in which Dante sees himself; the second is a rough black stone and across it run two cracks in the form of a cross; the third

> Seemed all of porphyry that flamed and shone
> Redder than bright blood spurting from a vein. . . .
>
>   (IX, 101–102)

The threshold itself, where the angel sits, is a rock of diamond.

The black, the white, and the red —they remind one of the nigredo, the albedo, and the rubedo of alchemy, which precede the finding of the "lapis," the "stone," often symbolized by the diamond. Here the white comes before the black, since in the Christian allegory the three steps stand for the three parts of the Sacrament of Penance—confession, contrition, and satisfaction; but on another level Dante's imagery may perhaps be said to foretell the state of modern man who must progress from the extreme clarity of his ego-consciousness into the darkness, from the white to the black, before he can find the red of sacrifice and love and mount from that onto the diamond threshold.

The white, the black, and the red: confession, contrition, satisfaction; first we must be willing to open our eyes and look at ourselves objectively in the mirror of the white stone, confessing openly to that which we see, as Dante did in the dark wood; secondly we must accept the "black," the journey into darkness where we shall be ground to pieces (the word "contrition" is derived from the Latin *tero*—"I grind"), until we emerge, as did the poet, onto the shores of the Mountain. Here the new attitude dawns, and the meaningless dismemberment of Hell becomes the Cross. Now as we approach the Gate of Peter we are initiated into the red, perhaps, even, as Dante was, through a dream, and are ready to embrace the passion, the fire of unremitting attention, the shedding of blood, which are the only means of "satisfaction." This is a powerful word; it comes from *satis*, "enough," and *facere*, "to make." When we realize that this is the true meaning of the penances suffered in Purgatory, we are at once freed from any false view of a penance as a retributive punishment. The experience of Purgatory in the psyche is the conscious suffering of the tension between the opposites until we know it is "enough" and are released from the swing between one extreme and the other into the "transcendent function," in Jung's phrase. This is the satisfaction, the at-one-ment, the becoming one.

"To him that knocketh it shall be opened"; but the knocking at Peter's Gate is not upon the door but upon the breast of the traveler himself.

> Devoutly falling at the holy feet
> I prayed him let me in for mercy's sake,
> But first upon my breast three times I beat.
>
> (IX, 109–111)

Fig. 24: Entrance into Purgatory

This is a reference to the ritual of Confession in the Church. The penitent knocks three times on his breast saying that he has sinned "by my fault, by my own fault, by my own most grievous fault." It symbolizes a man's objective acceptance of responsibility as a unique individual. Dante's use of the images here vividly reminds us that the Gate of Purgatory is in each man's own psyche, and when we know this we knock and the door is opened. Here in fact, as ritually in the confessional, all excuse-making is at an end; the blame for weakness or failure can no longer be laid at the door of fate or of our parents, of society, or of our circumstances. Paradoxically, this does not mean that we assume unbearable responsibility for all the darkness within; this, it will be remembered, was the great danger at the Gate of Dis. On the contrary, it means that we are *freed* from that burden of guilt in the moment when we take up our real responsibility—which is simply our own unceasing effort towards individual consciousness, towards maturity in love.

There is, moreover, another deep truth in these two lines:

I prayed him let me in for mercy's sake
But first upon my breast three times I beat.

(IX, 110–111)

When a man asserts his personal responsibility and his dignity as an individual, he is in no way claiming importance for his ego; on the contrary he is declaring that his ego with its narrow outlook is *not* the center of his personality. He does not knock on his head but on the center of his breast where, so to speak, the arms of the cross meet. He is asking for the gate to be opened, not because his ego deserves it or even wants it, but for *mercy's* sake. The taking up of individual responsibility, which is the acceptance of justice, of the scales, of the total commitment of Purgatory, is at the same moment on another level the recognition of The Mercy, which is all-forgiving compassion (a totally different thing from the blind pity which we often mistake for it). Until it is known and accepted, all effort towards justice remains a cold and sterile attempt to balance one opposite with another, without hope of the unity which unites and transcends them. How beautifully the two lines amplify the symbolism of Dante's dream! In it his ego accepted Justice and was plunged into the fire; but it was Lucy, the Lady of Mercy, who carried him up onto the threshold while he lay dreaming of the eagle. Awake now, though as yet he cannot see her, he asserts Mercy as the beginning and end of justice.

The angel now takes his sword and with its point writes the letter "P" seven times on Dante's forehead, and consciously he begins to pay. "P" here stands for *Peccatum*, the Latin word for sin. Each of the seven cornices of Purgatory is devoted to one of the seven deadly sins; and, as the poet emerges from one to the next, one of the letters is wiped away by an angel. Though there are certain parallels with the *Inferno*, the arrangement in the *Purgatorio* is on a different basis. The parallels are predominantly in the upper cornices which correspond with the upper circles of Hell—the realm of the lustful, for instance, being uppermost in both cases. But the first cornice of Purgatory, where live the shades of the proud, in no way corresponds to the deepest pit of Hell. There is no cornice for the fraudulent, the traitors, or the dishonest in Purgatory, for the obvious reason that these are conscious sinners; and no one who still consents to these evils can ever approach the Mountain at all. We know it well in our own terms—no one who is not prepared to be searchingly honest with himself can ever hope to begin on the way to individuation. The whole thing would be a lie and the pretender remains in his hell. The will is already redeemed on the threshold of Peter's Gate.

The sins purged on the Mountain are the instinctive forces in man which he has used for the pleasure or power of the ego and which have therefore fallen from their state of natural innocence and possessed him from the unconscious. Here man or woman struggles towards wholeness through the sacrifice of ego-power and concupiscence; and so the wolf, the lion, and the leopard, restored to their natural beauty, no longer block the path to the mountain top.

The doors to this realm are opened by the angel with his two keys. The golden one is turned with ease, but the silver

> . . . needs good stock
> Of wit and skill to get the bolt to stir,
> For that one grips the wards and frees the lock.
>   (IX, 124–126)

Dorothy Sayers writes of the allegory, "These are the two parts of absolution: The Golden Key is the Divine authority given to the Church to remit sin. . . . The Silver Key is the unloosening of the hard entanglement of sin in the human heart: and this needs great skill on the part of the Church and her priesthood when administering the sacrament of Penance."[12] Symbolically, gold is the metal of the sun, of consciousness; silver of the moon, the unconscious. The man who reaches this threshold has consented consciously to give all he has to the quest. His will is set as far as he controls it, and so the golden key freely turns. However, this is of no use without the "wit and skill" necessary to unravel and discriminate the hidden activity of his *un*conscious motivations. It is moreover the "angel" within who must finally do the unlocking, whether projected onto an outer guide or not; all our efforts, vital as they are, can do no more than bring us to the certainty that of ourselves we cannot add one cubit to our stature.

The attempt to do without one key or the other constantly bedevils religious and psychological thinking. The churches are apt to assert that the golden key of authority and of conscious good will is enough, while the psychologists proclaim the silver key as the "open sesame." Dante made no such mistake.

As he pushes open the door the angel speaks:

"Enter; but I must warn you: back outside
He goes, who looks behind him once he's passed."

(IX, 131–132)

Here Dante is speaking, not theologically of Purgatory after death, from which the shades never fall again, but directly of the purgatorial state on this earth. Any kind of looking back at this point will land one down in Ante-Purgatory again, if not in Hell, and the climb is harder each time.

The door swings open; not, as one might expect, smoothly and silently. On the contrary, the hinges "cried aloud . . . with . . . dreadful discord"; and then, mingling with the crashing of the gates, the song of Purgatory comes to Dante's ears.

Then, as I leaned, hearkening to that first sound,
Methought a voice sang, like some chorister's,
Te Deum laudamus, sweetly interwound

With music. . . .

(IX, 139–142)

So, standing there in the doorway, the mingling of the two sounds gives him a hint of what is to come—the transformation of all the clashing discords of the opposites at war into the single song of praise; he has entered the place where he is to discover the way of contemplation.

In religious terminology the phrases "contemplative life" and "active life" have a specific meaning, defining the emphasis on prayer or work in the various monastic orders. But contemplation is in fact an attitude to life, a way of relating to all phenomena, whether of the world outside or of the world within. To contemplate is to look at—and at the same time to reflect upon that which we see, with feeling as well as thought. There is no true contemplation without both detachment and involvement. For the most part men react partially to phenomena, to things, to people, to events, to themselves. Truly to look at and to see objectively, and so experience something in its wholeness, takes a very high level of awareness. All scientific observation demands long training and discipline, but this may be attained without involvement of the whole personality; not so contemplation, through which we may come to know fact and image, time and eternity, conscious and unconscious, in the smallest happenings of our lives. To put it another way: when we begin to contemplate, we are seeking to discern that which Jung called the Self, at the center of our lives, in place of the ego. In the East the mandala, which is the symbolic representation of this reality, was therefore the ritual object of religious contemplation; and, as Jung discovered, very many people today spontaneously produce mandala symbolism from their unconscious.

The souls in Dante's Purgatory are learning contemplation. On each cornice there are two kinds of images upon which they fix their inner gaze. On the one hand are examples of the wholeness which is born of an instinct redeemed; on the other, pictures of the deadliness of the instinct when it is in possession of the psyche. These pairs of opposites are called the Whip and the Bridle. We all know them as they come to us in dreams or imagination—the glowing possibilities for which we yearn and the dark opposite warning which saves us from hubris and restores the balance here in the dimensions of time and space. The images reach the souls on the Mountain in various ways. Either they are carved in the rock wall, or described by unseen voices, or imagined and spoken by the penitents themselves. The continuous contemplation of these

Fig. 25: The proud

things, however, is never an escape. Each soul is totally involved; and, while keeping his attention centered on the images of the opposites, he never ceases to be aware of the pain
which the tension between them brings. The proud are bowed
down under heavy stones, carrying the weight of the Self, as
they have attempted to usurp its power; the envious sit with
sealed eyes, having been unable to rejoice in the sight of beauty
or goodness in others; the slothful run without a moment's
pause. So we, to whatever extreme we swing consciously,
must come to know the opposite which is gripping us in the
unconscious by giving unwavering attention to the images
which rise up from the depths to warn or to point the way.

The white, the black, the red, and the certainty of the
diamond, a rock beneath his feet—all are here as Dante crosses
the threshold and moves onto the spiral way.

The Approach to the Fire

WITHIN THE GATE, the poets now move on and climb from one cornice to another towards the searing fire through which every man must finally pass before he emerges again into the lost innocence of Eden, this time as a unique and conscious individual.

Purgatory has three divisions. On the lower three terraces are the proud, the envious, and the wrathful—those whose love has been egocentrically perverted and who have willed harm to others. Of these and their penances we have already spoken. On the fourth level are the slothful and the careless, whose love was inadequate and weak. On the upper three cornices the covetous, the gluttonous, and the lustful—those who would not put first things first—are purged of disordered and possessive love. Between each of the cornices (ledges eighteen feet wide) there is a steep stairway cut into the rock, each guarded by an angel. It is significant that on four of the ledges Dante is an observer merely, while on the other three— the cornices of pride, wrath, and lust—he briefly joins the souls in their suffering. He thus confesses to his own shadow side.

The journey takes two days. On the evening of the first, Dante and Virgil, having looked upon the images of the opposites on the first three cornices and having talked with individuals of their suffering and their joy, now climb the stairway to the terrace of the slothful.

Sloth, says Dorothy Sayers, "is not merely idleness of mind and laziness of body: it is that whole poisoning of the will which, beginning with indifference and an attitude of "I couldn't care less," extends to the deliberate refusal of joy and culminates in morbid introspection and despair."[13] Here are the permissive, the so-called "disillusioned" for whom everything is "nothing but," and the escapists. We may add to this list the impatient and those who live in a constant state of hurry. This is in fact an inverted state of sloth, a refusal of the hard work of consenting to the present moment. The cornice of sloth is the central point of Purgatory and most aptly so, for our battle with this insidious enemy extends upwards and downwards throughout the journey. It creeps up on us in many and various forms, often unrecognized. We procrastinate, we have no time, we are continuously "busy," we indulge in "nothing buts" disguised as humility, we demand immediate results; and all these things are just plain sloth.

The sun is sinking, and by the law of the mountain the poets may not move at night. They sit, and now at the exact center, not only of Purgatory but of the entire poem, Virgil instructs Dante on the nature of love and free will, as far as human reason and understanding can define it. He stresses, however, that only through Beatrice, beyond all rational concepts, can Dante come to true awareness of these things.

Dante never devalues the lesser because it is incomplete and must finally be transcended. He expresses this explicitly, as we shall see, in Virgil's last words to him at the top of the mountain. The tenderness and beauty of this whole treatment of the figure of Virgil is a shining example. Courtesy and respect are shown to the great pagan by all the redeemed souls—and the poets among them express their humble love and reverence. Virgil is not degraded because he must return below to Limbo; he remains forever an essential part of the whole. So here, while Dante is aware that in Heaven he will know love by direct experience, he gives his whole attention to the definitions of human reason, accepting the inevitable risk of temporary overevaluation of the intellect. For without the full exercise of all our faculties the great experience will never come.

The contemptuous rejection of one value and the exclusive exaltation of another has been for centuries the extreme peril, and today in our present counter-culture the danger is identical. We have seen the supremacy of reason and intellect and the repression of the irrational produce an unbearable sterility; and now in the powerful swing-over to the values of instinct and emotion, the responsibility of objective thought is, in its turn, in danger of violent rejection. This is the inner meaning of heresy—the adherence to one truth at the expense of, instead of in relation to, its opposite. One could call it the refusal of paradox.

It is therefore no surprise that Dante, almost immediately after listening to the golden voice of Virgil discoursing on love,

Fig. 26: The dream of the siren

should fall asleep and have a very ugly dream about the voice of the Siren. We may imagine him growing drowsy in a glow of exaltation, uplifted by the beauty of Virgil's words, feeling himself aware now of what love is; and then comes the comment from the unconscious, the balancing opposite, the warning that, if he is carried away into overevaluation of reason, he will be in acute danger of being possessed by the voice of the devouring anima promising all knowledge and all delight if he will give himself to her. Here is the dream:

> In dream a woman sought me, halt of speech,
> Squint-eyed, on maimed feet lurching as she stept,
> With crippled hands, and skin of sallowy bleach.

> I gazed; and as to cold limbs that have crept
> Heavy with night, the sun gives life anew,
> Even so my look unloosed the string that kept

> Her utterance captive, and right quickly drew
> Upright her form that all misshapen hung,
> And stained her withered cheek to love's own hue.

Then she began to sing, when thus her tongue
Was freed—and such a spell she held me by
As had been hard to break; and so she sung:

"Lo, the sweet Siren! yea, 'tis I, 'tis I
Who lead the mariners in mid-sea astray,
Such pleasures in my melting measures lie.

I turned Ulysses from his wandering way
With music; few, I trow, to me who grow
Know how to go, longing I so allay."

Her lips yet moved to that melodious flow
When hard at hand a lady I espied,
Holy, alert, her guiles to overthrow.

"O Virgil, Virgil, who is this?" she cried
Indignant; and he came, with heedful eyes
On that discreet one, and on naught beside.

The first he seized, and, rending her disguise
In front, showed me her belly, which released
So foul a stench, I woke with that surprise.

I looked about for my good lord: "At least
Three times," said he, "I've called thee; rise and come. . . ."

(XIX, 7–35)

As in all great dreams, every detail here is alive with meaning. Most commentators point out the allegory—the Siren as the personification of the sins of concupiscence, purged on the three upper terraces which Dante is about to enter. Dorothy Sayers as usual goes deeper. She calls the Siren the "magical fantasm of man's own desire," "a devouring egotistical fantasy by absorption in which the personality rots away into illusion"—the succubus, in fact.[14] But no one I know of has stressed the extreme importance of the dream as the reply of the unconscious to the dangers of an overevaluation of the reasoned discourse which preceded it.

Forgetting, it seems, Virgil's words of warning, "So much as reason here distinguisheth I can unfold . . . ; thereafter sound Beatrice's mind alone," Dante says, "So I, who'd reaped succinct and luminous replies to all my questions, could relax in rambling thoughts. . . ." The meeting with the shades of the slothful intervenes here with obvious meaning, and as soon as they have passed he returns to his satisfied musing.

. . . there rose
New fancies in my mind, whence thick and fast

Sprang others, countless, various; and from those
To these I drifted, down so long a stream
Of rambling thought, my lids began to close,

And meditation melted into dream.
>   (XVIII, 140–145)

It is a perfect description of what happens the moment we imagine that because everything is clear in the head, all is accomplished. At the least *abaissement du niveau mental*, clear reason turns to lazy rambling thoughts which merge into sexual fantasies and the voice of the Siren.

To Dante, however, comes the saving dream, making absolutely clear, in vivid imagery, the danger, its cause, and its cure. A woman approaches him, horribly ugly and distorted—an image of what happens to the feeling side of man when he forgets the values of relatedness and despises the feminine and irrational in the pride of his intellect and reason. But the despised thing in the unconscious acquires magical power. She holds the fascinated gaze of the dreamer, for with her a large part of man's libido may be imprisoned in the unconscious; and sooner or later if he makes no effort towards consciousness, this libido, his preoccupation, his involuntary "gaze" will transform her into a thing so alluring, so seemingly beautiful, that he passes completely into her power. A man under the spell of the Siren is at the mercy of every mood, quite incapable of seeing an actual woman except through a haze of projections or collective rationalizations, unable to sacrifice any of his emotional impulses to the value of a true feeling response; and meanwhile his rambling thoughts are mistaken for real consciousness, a delusion of which the Siren constantly sings. The end is, of course, that she tears him to pieces and eats him on her island of escape from life, as we are told in the *Odyssey*, and the "personality rots away into illusion." Such is the anima-possessed man.

"Why Dante," we may ask in astonishment, "who of all people gave full value to feeling, to the feminine?" I think the dream is a clear instance of the truth that the more conscious a man becomes, the more dangerous are his lapses, small though they may appear. Moreover, it is almost certain that the temptations of philosophy and of allegory without symbol, as substitutes for the "feeling intellect," had been great in Dante's earlier life. A prolonged relapse at this high point on the mountain would indeed have been perilous. The release and awakening, however, come almost immediately in the dream. A woman, "holy and alert"—whole and conscious— appears, and her voice breaks the spell. What follows is an example of how a dream may condense a whole world of meaning into one brief image. The lady is a symbol of real, mature feeling, and she calls upon Virgil, image of the best and wisest human reason, to reveal to Dante the nature of his delusion. Virgil strips off the Siren's disguise, but while he does it, he gazes steadily at the true woman (Dante's actual words are *"quella onesta"*—"that honest one"). Then Dante through his instinctive sense of smell is awakened and set free. What could more powerfully assert the equal value of human thought, feeling, and instinct, all three? A man has the power to unmask delusion through his clear thinking as long as, but only as long as, his eyes are fixed on the truth of feeling; moreover it is very clear that the woman alone would have been powerless and that neither would have broken the spell on the dreamer without the cooperation of his own instinct, his "nose" for the truth. "Wake up," says the dream to Dante. "Wake up to the horror which would swallow you if you were to forget the mind of Beatrice." Beatrice rejected becomes the "ancient witch" who promises man all knowledge and all pleasure without any of the suffering and hard work of learning relatedness and love; but rooted in feeling, you will hear with your whole being the words of Virgil revealing truth to your mind.

It is interesting at this point to look back and remember that, just as here at the center of Purgatory Dante meets the image of the witch-like Siren, so halfway down the circles of Hell he had been confronted with the same threat from the devouring feminine in the much more dangerous form of Medusa's head. There, as here, everything hangs on "looking"; but there, to have looked would have destroyed him, whereas here, in his much more differentiated state of consciousness, his gaze, though a great danger, is nevertheless a means to a new clear-eyed awakening.

> "A strange, disturbing dream, I cannot ban
> From out my mind, has set me in a scare,"
> Said I, "and makes me only half a man."

> "Saw'st thou that ancient witch, for whose sole snare
> The mount above us weeps? and how one deals
> With her," he answered, "and is rid of her?"
>
> (XIX, 55–60)

And Virgil urges Dante to look up at "the great celestial wheels" whose "lure" will wholly banish the power of the Siren. Thus he confirms the message of the dream; it is the direction of his *gaze* which must now, in this place of training for contemplation which is Purgatory, be Dante's one concern. Only a greater lure can cure a lesser; one desire yields only to another, never to reason, until all desires are transcended. Dante's gaze at the Siren was the only thing that gave her power; Virgil's gaze at the lady defeated this power; and now Dante, setting his eyes firmly on the great celestial wheels (which are an inner image of wholeness) is strong enough to climb to the next stairway, to take the next small step.

It is a great transition point, in spite of the fact that here there is no obvious outer barrier to be crossed. Virgil's discourse, as has been said, comes at the center of the whole poem; and there follows the dream through which we feel that Dante is finally freed from the lure of the Siren. The threatened split between thinking and feeling is healed, the cornice of sloth, the danger of drifting into "random thoughts" is left behind. Moreover, when Dante looks up at the celestial wheels, the fourth function is joined to the other three and confirms his freedom. Thinking, feeling, and sensation were all at work in the dream, and now through imaginative intuition he glimpses the goal.[15]

So the sun rises on Dante, "without and within"; he sets out on the last day of his quest for Beatrice.

> Like to a hawk, that sits with folded wing,
> Eyeing its feet, and at the call turns swift,
> Eager for food, wings spread to soar and swing,
>
> Such I became; and so, right through the rift
> One climbs by, up to where the shelf runs round
> Once more, did I my cheerful flight uplift.
>
> (XIX, 64–69)

Here, I would like to digress and say a little about the parallel experience through which a woman may pass. What is the equivalent of the Siren for her? It is a question of immense importance for every woman, especially at this moment of history.

The dominance of masculine values through so many centuries has had a doubly dangerous effect on the psyche of woman. Man despises his inferior feminine side, but woman has learnt to despise her own dominant value, the femininity which is the center of her being. This attitude persists in the unconscious long after it has changed consciously. There are many women who project the feminine values onto trivial vanities or onto what they call domestic drudgery. Thus they identify womanhood with a despised aspect of the anima of man and never recognize at all their true identity as carriers of relatedness, feeling values, and the quiet nourishing qualities of the earth.

In order to find her freedom and release her own positive masculine creative spirit, she has a double task: she must discover what it really means to be a woman at the same time as she brings up and relates to the masculine in her unconscious. The equivalent for her of the lure of the Siren in a man's unconscious is therefore the glittering image of power through identification with a masculine type of activity which swallows up her womanhood; she is dazzled by second-hand concepts and by the spell of words. This is not to say that she cannot work on equal terms with man in fields which have been considered specifically his; on the contrary, every conscious woman *needs* to do some so-called masculine work. But if she works in imitation of man instead of out of her own nature, she will be identified with an inferior kind of masculinity, inevitably sterile because it is based on a rejection of the core of her being. She too, then, is in the grip of the incubus, is devoured by an image, as man is by the Siren, until "the personality rots away into illusion." Many women today, reacting violently against the age-long degradation of the feminine, proclaim quite rightly the equality of woman with man on the level of value and ability, and her need to be freed from the contempt which has sought to confine her to conventional roles; but too often they try to achieve their goals by an attempt to obliterate all difference in the human nature of man and woman. The result is, of course, a far worse kind of contempt—the rejection of one half of reality itself and the submergence of the individual woman into the meaninglessness of imitation. Thus all the true freedom and creativeness of her spirit is lost.

At the other end of the scale, of course, this kind of imitation produces the very thing it rejects, and unconsciously the woman caught in it becomes a mere prostitute inwardly, if not outwardly, since her instinctual life is separated from her true creative task of nourishing responsible relationship.

For both men and women, then, at this point half-way up the mountain of consciousness comes a moment of great temptation—the temptation to drift into the easy way of identification with Siren or glittering animus. For both the saving image is the same—the mind and heart of Beatrice, that mature human feeling united to deep reflection which finally brings us to the point where we may, if we are steadfast, intuit the unknown center which is love itself.

Here at the center of the *Commedia*, I will quote in part Virgil's discourse on love and free will, and then set beside these some words of C.G. Jung in our day.

> . . . "Never, my son, was yet
> Creator, no, nor creature, without love
> Natural or rational—and thou knowest it.
>
> The natural cannot make an erring move;
> The other may, either by faulty aim
> Or else by too much zeal or lack thereof.
>
> When to the great prime goods it makes full claim,
> Or to the lesser goods in measure due,
> No sin can come of its delight in them;
> . . . .
>
> The soul, which is created apt for love,
> The moment pleasure wakes it into act,
> To any pleasant thing is swift to move.
>
> Your apprehension draws from some real fact
> An inward image, which it shows to you,
> And by that image doth the soul attract:
> . . . .
>
> So the enamoured soul falls to desire—
> A motion spiritual—nor rest can find
> Till its loved object it enjoy entire.
>
> Now canst thou see how wholly those are blind
> To truth, who think all love is laudable
> Just in itself, no matter of what kind,

. . . .

Grant, then, all loves that wake in you to be
Born of necessity, you still possess
Within yourselves the power of mastery;

And this same noble faculty it is
Beatrice calls Free Will. . . .

. . . .

So much as reason here distinguisheth
I can unfold," said he; "thereafter sound
Beatrice's mind alone, for that needs faith."

(XVII, 91–99; XVIII, 19–74)

And Jung, speaking out of both reason and the "mind of Beatrice," wrote, "Love requires depth and loyalty of feeling: without them it is not love but mere caprice. True love will always commit itself and engage in lasting ties; it needs freedom only to effect its choice, not for its accomplishment. . . . Love has more than one thing in common with religious faith. It demands unconditional trust and expects absolute surrender."[16] In the beautiful ending of *Memories, Dreams, and Reflections* he says of love, as does Dante, that its "range of activity extends from the endless spaces of the heavens to the dark abysses of hell." Love is, he continues, ". . . something superior to the individual, a unified and undivided whole. Being a part, a man cannot grasp the whole. He is at its mercy. He may assent to it, or rebel against it; but he is always caught up by it and enclosed within it. He is dependent upon it and is sustained by it. Love is his light and his darkness, whose end he cannot see. 'Love ceases not'—whether he speaks with the 'tongues of angels,' or with scientific exactitude traces the life of the cell down to its uttermost source. Man can try to name love, showering upon it all the names at his command, and still he will involve himself in endless self-deceptions. If he possesses a grain of wisdom he will lay down his arms and name the unknown by the more unknown *ignotum per ignotius*— that is, by the name of God. That is a confession of his subjection, his imperfection, and his dependence; but at the same time a testimony to his freedom to choose between truth and error."[17] This is indeed the theme of the *Commedia* from first to last.

The Passage of the Fire

O N THE THREE UPPER cornices are the souls of the covetous, the gluttonous, and the lustful, those caught in the three aspects of that possessive love which feeds the desire of the ego instead of nourishing the Self. Having talked with one of the covetous, the poets are halted and stupefied by a totally unexpected experience. The whole mountain shakes as with a tremendous earthquake, and there follows a great glad cry from every soul in Purgatory, "*Gloria in excelsis Deo.*" Both poets are pale with the shock. "Never," says Dante, "with such frantic lust for learning did any ignorance in my life assail me." His curiosity is soon laid to rest, for the travelers are hailed by the soul of the poet Statius, who explains to them that he has just been released from Purgatory into bliss and says that, although the mountain above Peter's Gate is never shaken by the forces of nature, yet,

"But when some spirit, feeling purged and sound,
Leaps up or moves to seek a loftier station,
The whole mount quakes and the great shouts resound.

The will itself attests its own purgation;
Amazed, the soul that's free to change its inn
Finds its mere will suffice for liberation;

True, it wills always, but can nothing win
So long as heavenly justice keeps desire
Set toward the pain as once 'twas towards the sin. . . ."
(XXI, 58–66)

If we were still looking for proof of Dante's profound psychological wisdom, these lines would leave us in no doubt. Many times it comes to us in lesser degree along the way—this sense of sudden release from an inner conflict which has long absorbed our energy—and the amazement with which we know ourselves "free to change our inn," to seek new ground upon which to stand. There is no hint at all of an arbitrary external

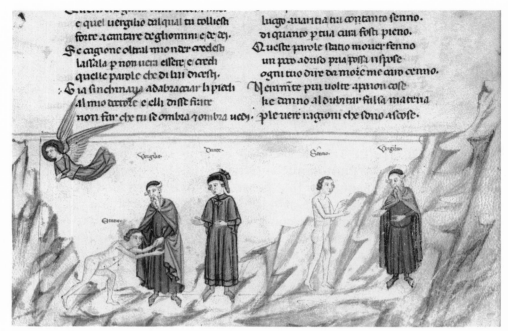

Fig. 27: The avaricious and the prodigal; Statius

deity setting a man free after he has punished him long enough—"The will itself attests its own purgation." However great our desire for it, the will does not really *want* freedom until we have borne the tension and the conflict long enough to purge us of all demand for this or that. The pain of this bondage to the split within us is the "heavenly justice" to which the man who has accepted Purgatory gives his allegiance. So, although from the beginning we want freedom from conflict, we do not desire with a whole heart to be released into Mercy, into Love; and this whole heart can be born in us only when the human state of conflict is accepted.

There follows a passage which touches the heart of true courtesy. Statius, the released and redeemed soul, speaks of his love for Virgil, and Dante smiles—almost winks—so that Statius questions him and finds that Virgil is actually there beside him. Statius falls to his knees and would stoop to kiss the beloved pagan's feet, so that Virgil has to remind him they are shades. Any description is clumsy and does not convey the delicate beauty of the incident. The three now travel on together towards the summit.

On the last cornice they come to the fire. "On the Blissful

Mountain," says Dorothy Sayers, "the traditional 'Purgatory Fire' is conspicuous by its absence: only on its last and highest and most triumphant Cornice does this great Scriptural image blaze out with a sudden splendid lucidity. . . . Fire, which is an image of Lust, is also an image of Purity. The burning of the sin, and the burning charity which is its opposing virtue, here coalesce into a single image and a single experience. . . ."[18]

> Here the bank belches forth great sheets of flame,
> While upward from the cornice edge doth blow
> A blast that shields it, backward bending them,
>
> So that in single file we had to go,
> Where space allowed; and I was sore afraid,
> On this side, fire—on that, the depths below.
>
> "This is a place," my leader therefore said,
> "Where wandering eyes a strict control require,
> Since a false step were all too easy made."
>
> (XXV, 112–120)

"Wandering eyes" were here no longer a harmless lapse; the direction of the inner gaze has become the one wholly essential thing. All wandering desires and fears, all opposites of what-

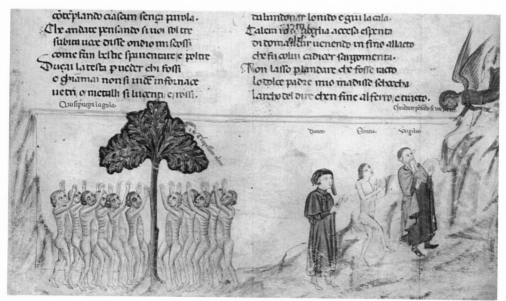

Fig. 28: The gluttonous

ever kind are gathered into the intensity of looking; images and experience have become a single reality.

Dante looks deep into the fire and sees the souls of those being purged of natural and unnatural lust running in opposite directions around the mountain—and as they pass, each greets another with a kiss. Thus the journey between damnation and salvation begins and ends with a kiss. Paolo and Francesca at the beginning of the *Inferno* kiss and begin the slide into unconscious identification and the betrayal of love which is the kiss of Judas. The souls here at the threshold of freedom kiss in that conscious exchange of human love which is the door to salvation and wholeness.

It is interesting that in the *Inferno* the sodomites are placed far down in the City of Dis, whereas the heterosexual lustful are in the topmost circle where their pains are far less deadly. In contrast to this, here in Purgatory both kinds of lust are purged together on the highest cornice. It is another example of Dante's great insight. A homosexual who falls into promiscuity and indiscriminate lust is usually in a far worse state of ego-centered neurosis and disintegration than a heterosexual in a similar case; but a man who has accepted his homosexual tendency, whatever its psychological causes, and has embraced the pain of transforming it into conscious love, burns in the fire on equal terms with those who suffer from "natural" lust. The reason for this lies in the fact that the desire for a person of the same sex exposes a man or woman far more dangerously to the horrors of auto-erotic isolation than the desire for the opposite sex, however promiscuous. Even the most sordid lust between the sexes is at least some sort of reaching out for the "other" within, whereas the desire of man for man, or woman for woman, when all effort towards responsible love is abandoned, much more easily becomes a turning in of the personality upon itself until all the values of human exchange are destroyed. When once, however, that effort and the sacrifice it involves are accepted, all are equal upon the way; for each and every love, no matter what or whom its object, is recognized as a reflection, however dim, of the love of that Other which is the Self. Slowly we move towards the realization of this love, transcendent and immanent, until we burn in the fire and are free.

Every thought and act derives from love of some kind, says Dante, whether distorted into self-destroying desire, or redeemed into conscious, creative exchange. In Jung's words, love's activity ranges from "the endless spaces of the heavens to the dark abysses of Hell," and we are free to choose. Therefore, on this highest cornice *all* souls must make the final choice and pass through the fire, whether their specific sin has been lust or not.

Dante, walking carefully along the edge, has not yet realized this. As with most of us the moment comes with a shock of terror. The fear of his dream of the eagle now becomes consciously confronted fear. He sees the glory of the angel standing on the further side of the fire and rejoices in the beauty of his voice singing, "Blessed are the pure in heart." Then the angel speaks to the travelers:

> . . . "Holy souls, there's no way on or round
> But through the bite of fire; in, then, and come!
> Nor be you deaf to what is sung beyond."
>
> As we approached him, thus his words struck home;
> And it was so with me when this I heard
> Even as with one who's carried to the tomb.
>
> I leaned across my clasped hands, staring hard
> Into the fire, picturing vividly
> Sights I had seen, of bodies burned and charred.
>   (XXVII, 10–18)

Virgil and Statius both turn to strengthen him—and Virgil reasons gently, assuring him that he cannot die in this fire, for it is the fire which burns but does not consume. He even invites him to hold a bit of his tunic in the fire so as to prove to himself that it will remain intact. But, as at the beginning of the journey, so here at the last barrier of Purgatory, no reasoning, however convincing, can help Dante, or indeed any of us.

> "Have done with fear henceforth, have done with it—
> Turn and go safe." And there was I, for all
> My conscience smote me, budging ne'er a whit.
>   (XXVII, 31–33)

Only the name of Beatrice gives him the courage to go on, as it had given him the courage to start out of the dark wood of the beginning. Only love, actual and incarnate on this earth, personal as well as impersonal, can take us through the fire which burns away desire and fear.

. . . "Look, my son," he said,
"'Twixt Beatrice and thee there is this wall."

. . .

So did I turn me to my leader wise,
My hardness melting at the name which aye
Like a fresh well-spring in my heart doth rise.
        (XXVII, 35–42)

So Virgil went into the fire, talking still of Beatrice waiting for
him on the other side, and so coaxing and cheering him on.
Dante followed.

And I, being in, would have been glad to throw
Myself for coolness into molten glass,
With such unmeasured heat did that fire glow.
        (XXVII, 49–51)

As they come out of the fire, night is falling once again. There
is a last stairway through a cleft in the rock up to the summit
of the mountain. They start up it, but, as the sun sets, they lie
down, each upon a stair. Gazing up between the high rock
walls, Dante looks upon the stars shining "bigger and brighter
than they'd ever been."

Ruminant thus I gazed on them afar
Until sleep took me—sleep that oft in dreams
Can give us news of things before they are.
        (XXVII, 91–93)

Dante is no longer in danger of drifting off into random
thoughts and fantasies. His gaze is sure and steady; he rumi-
nates, contemplates, and the dream which comes to him is
very simple. He sees the images of two ladies; one, young and
beautiful, is picking flowers in a meadow to deck herself with
so that she may enjoy her image in the glass. She is Leah. And
Rachel, her sister, sits still before her mirror. Leah and Rachel
often represented the active and contemplative lives respectively in medieval allegory, and Leah tells Dante in his dream
that such is their meaning. But, as usual, Dante never stops
at mere allegory. The interesting thing about the dream is that
both sisters look into the mirror at themselves, the difference

being that Rachel looks into her own eyes, her own depths, all the time seeing therein the microcosm of all things; while Leah looks first outward on the beauty of flowers and then uses her hands to unite that beauty to herself. What a very different attitude to the active life from our own! Both the active and the contemplative ways have become a *looking*. Rachel looks inward, Leah looks outward, but both look at themselves. In Dante's brief vision of Leah we feel the transformation of action by looking—looking deeply into the core of every act, every object until the light of the unity shines into our eyes from the ten thousand things and out again into the world. There is said to be an inscription on a gravestone in Cumberland, England, which reads, "The wonder of the world, the beauty, and the power, the shape of things, their colors, lights and shades, these I saw. Look ye also while life lasts."

Each sister has found her identity; each sees in the mirror herself, objectively, cleansed of all personal vanity, because the self she sees is also the Self—inner and outer are one.

So the sun rises and the poets climb the long stair. "At every step I felt my feet grow wings." On the top stair Virgil turns to Dante for the last time. The purgation is over; Dante is free "to love and do as he wills." Virgil's own words alone suffice here.

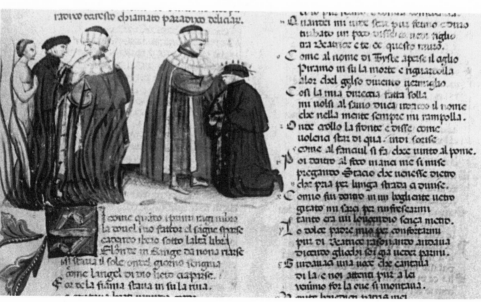

Fig. 29: "I mitre thee and crown."

. . . "The temporal fire and the eterne
Thou hast beheld, my son, and reached a place
Where, of myself, no further I discern.

I've brought thee here by wit and by address;
Make pleasure now thy guide—thou art well sped
Forth of the steep, forth of the narrow ways.

See how the sun shines here upon thy head;
See the green sward, the flowers, the boskages
That from the soil's own virtue here are bred.

While those fair eyes are coming, bright with bliss,
Whose tears sent me to thee, thou may'st prospect
At large, or sit at ease to view all this.

No word from me, no further sign expect;
Free, upright, whole, thy will henceforth lays down
Guidance that it were error to neglect,

Whence o'er thyself I mitre thee and crown.

(XXVII, 127–142)

The Passage of the Waters

Eager to search, in and throughout its ways
The sacred wood, whose thick and leafy tent,
Spread in my sight, tempered the new sun's rays,

I made no pause, but left the cliff and went
With lingering steps across the level leas
Where all the soil breathed out a fragrant scent.

        (XXVIII, 1–6)

DANTE HIMSELF now leads the way, though Virgil has not yet left him, and the three poets move into the sacred wood of the Earthly Paradise. All through these cantos Dante refers to Eden not as a garden, as one might expect, but as a forest. Inevitably we remember, and are surely meant to remember, the dark and threatening wood in which Dante had been lost. There is, we sense, only one wood. Split off from our true identity, stumbling about in the fogs of pride and desire, the innocent forest of the unconscious is dark and destructive to us, and its paths lead down into despair; but here at the summit of human consciousness, "free, whole and upright," a man finds the forest again—the strength and beauty of the great trees thrusting up from the fragrant soil, the grateful shade of the branches, the rustling of the leaves in the gentle wind, and the singing of the birds.

  . . . they welcomed with rejoicing song
The dawn-wind to the leaves. . . .

        (XXVIII, 16–17)

Thus it is with all the archetypes—with all the life of nature for that matter—nature outside or within is innocent both in its dark and its light aspects. It is the attitude, the degree of wholeness in each human being which determines the impact upon him.

Fig. 30: The Earthly Paradise; Matilda

Here is the place of the unconscious innocence of the beginning and of infancy, from which all men fall, or grow, into the darkness of ignorance and conflict and to which Dante has returned through greater darkness and the climb to the purging fire. Dante's Earthly Paradise is empty of human beings, for no man dwells there since Adam and Eve "fell" into the quest for consciousness. For those who make the return it is now merely a place of passage—a gateway to the stars. For the conscious return takes us far beyond the state of natural innocence.

So Dante walks through the ancient wood and comes to a little river, whose water is so clear that, he says, "whatso waters over here we call clearest, were cloudy by comparison," and looking across the stream he sees

A lady all alone, who wandered there
Singing and plucking flower on floweret gay,
With which her path was painted everywhere.
(XXVIII, 40–42)

This lady is one of the most enchanting people in the *Commedia*. Wise and beautiful, full of grace and courtesy, she sparkles with gaiety and wit—she is the forerunner sent to bring Dante to Beatrice; and it is she, as we shall see, who leads him through the waters of the twin rivers of Lethe and Eunoe—indeed she drags him through the first! The commentators say briefly that she represents the Active Life, and indeed it is obvious that Leah in Dante's dream is the image behind her; but because Dante's figures are all identifiable people, actual or mythological, there has been a great deal of speculation about her. Later Beatrice casually calls her by name, Matilda. Dorothy Sayers surmises that she was probably a friend of Beatrice's in Florence whom Dante knew by name, and it seems a likely guess. Matilda is one of the most vivid examples of what happens to cold allegory under the magic of Dante's vision. Matilda, we say rightly, stands for the Active Life, but then we laugh at the absurdity of that bald statement. Matilda is Matilda, a unique and fascinating woman who makes an immediate personal impact on Dante and on every reader; and it is because of this that we really do glimpse through her the dancing beauty at the core of all true activity. So we may understand better Jung's insistence that until a concept or a feeling or an attitude is personified—confronted in the image of a person, through projection or dream or imagination—no "taking thought"can change the psyche. If we were to think of Matilda as the Active Life, and leave it at that, we might as well stop reading the poem altogether since we would certainly be bored by all that follows; for the person Matilda is a forerunner of the person who is Beatrice.

Dante, watching her, is reminded of Persephone, and calls to her, begging her to come to the edge of the stream so that he may hear the words of her song. "As a dancing lady turns with her toes together. . . . So she to me." Standing facing him across the water, Matilda answers Dante's questions about the forest, and tells him of the two rivers which spring from a single fountain. This one is Lethe, the water of oblivion, and by drinking it a man's sins are blotted from his memory; but later, on the other side of the Forest, he will drink of Eunoe, and his memory will return. The word *Eunoe* means "good mind," and it is not known whether Dante invented it or found it in some lost classical text. When we drink of this stream, sin will no longer be forgotten but forgiven—that is, will be fully remembered not as shameful and destructive but as a *felix culpa*, the experience of darkness essential to wholeness: "O happy fault that wert the occasion of so great a redemption."

It is not time, however, for Dante to pass through Lethe. On either bank the lady and the poets move upstream, and soon they hear music. The Pageant of the Sacrament, as Dorothy Sayers calls it, approaches on Matilda's side of the river. "For the great focal point of the *Commedia*—the reunion of Dante with Beatrice—is deliberately set, as though upon a stage, between two great pageants or masques, in which the characters are not *symbolic personages* but *allegorical personifications* in the traditional manner, embodying abstract ideas. . . . The persons are still actual existent beings, as all actors are existent beings; but they are actors, and they are presenting a show."[19] It may seem strange to us that Dante should desert symbol for allegory at the approach to his supreme moment; but, in fact, the impact of it—of his meeting with the great transforming symbol of his life who was both inner image and actual person—is enormously enhanced by this stage setting. Also, we must remember that allegory, no matter how obviously it represents abstract ideas to the conscious mind, at once becomes symbolic when it touches associations in the unconscious. The great rituals with which men have always surrounded the enactment of the central mystery of life are of this nature. In the Christian Mass there is a long preparation for the moment of revelation— a *rite d'entrée*—designed to open the conscious mind and the feeling heart and also to touch the numinous images in the unconscious of a man, so that the revelation may be an experience as total as is possible to him. Every detail of the ritual is pregnant with meaning on all levels. Allegorically one can say of each one such things as "This means purity," "This means repentance," and so on; and from the color of the vestments to the chalice itself, everything may yield a wealth of association to conscious and unconscious. But at the moment of the consecration of the bread and wine, the words are not "This means my body and blood," but "This *is* my Body and Blood," and there follows a silence and a showing forth. So, as we shall see, it is with the coming of Beatrice.

Dante gazes across the river entranced, as the head of the procession comes into view. For him, and his contemporaries, this was no frigid allegorical show; nor need it be so for us if we do not become enmeshed in the enumeration of the abstract representations, but rather yield ourselves to the poetry and the images. The twenty-four elders stand for the books of the Old Testament; the three shimmering ladies, white, green, and red, represent Faith, Hope, and Charity; the Gryphon is a figure of the double nature of Christ, divine and human. All this we may know, but at the moment of entering into Dante's vision with our *imagination*, we too may watch with enchanted wonder, as he did, the blazing of the fire from the seven-branched candlesticks; the dignity of the old men; the grace and joy of the dancing maidens; and the glory of the rainbow-colored light that filled the sky. And we too may feel awe as the Gryphon appears with its eagle head and wings of gold and its red and white animal body, drawing behind it the empty chariot.

> The wings rose higher than my sight could see;
> Golden of limb so far as he was bird,
> The rest all dappled red-and-white was he.
>
> Rome upon Africanus ne'er conferred
> Nor on Augustus' self, a car so brave—
> Nay, but the sun's own car were poor, compared. . . .
>
> (XXIX, 112–117)

Nevertheless, all this remains a collective, impersonal ritual and is meant to be so in order to throw into startling relief the intensely personal nature of the central figure of the whole. We see the triumphal car of the Church, standing for the altar without and within, upon which the eternal mystery is shown forth in time; we expect a symbol of the Sacrament; and Dante in this moment of high drama dared to say in effect to every man, "The Sacrament of the altar is that image, that reality, which in you personally has awakened love and total devotion on every level of your being—body, soul, mind, and spirit. This is in truth the birth of Christ within and can lead you to the unity which is both center and circumference. Beatrice, standing on the car, both plays the part and *is* the Sacrament itself."

If we can imagine for a moment Dante standing beside the river and seeing Beatrice approaching without any of the poetry and drama of the masque, we will, I think, realize that it would have been very hard for him or for his readers in any age to experience the power and mystery of her double nature. We could think about her divine meaning just as well and feel deep emotion at Dante's personal reunion with her, but the single vision would elude almost all. The medieval rituals have long been dying in the West, and they no longer evoke the numinous in the unconscious of most people. We know too much about them in the head, as Jung said. The Catholic Church long maintained them through the great poetry and visual beauty of the old rites, but these things are now in

Fig. 31: *The Earthly Paradise; pageant of the Church; Beatrice*

process of being replaced by everyday talk, emotional music, ordinary dress, vessels, and surroundings. The movement surely springs from a growing consciousness of the great truth proclaimed by Dante—the truth that the Sacrament is not something received exclusively in Church but is to be experienced through each individual's "god-bearing" images in daily life. But we are in danger of losing sight of man's basic need of a ritual, a numinous *rite d'entrée* to this very mystery.

Since most of us can no longer experience it in a collective rite, each must therefore find for himself the images which awake a numinous response. They may come to us through nature, art, or relationship, through dreams, or through scientific truth, provided always that we never mistake the means for the end, and that we recognize in them the symbol which stirs to life an intuition of the mystery.

One example of a true scientist, in whose works we feel that the very precision of his observation is a doorway opening continually onto the mystery, is Loren Eisely. Another was, of course, Teilhard de Chardin. Anything, anything at all, can be a doorway for us the moment it expands into poetry.

In awe Dante watches the Gryphon halt. The car is empty and the moment for which, hearts beating with his, we have waited, is upon us. A great shout rises from all the actors in the drama, "*Benedictus qui venis,*" "Blessed art thou that comest."

The third person of this hymn has been changed to the second. Dorothy Sayers writes, ". . . and it is particularly noteworthy that, although that which 'comes' is Beatrice, Dante has retained unaltered the masculine ending in -us, which refers it definitely to Christ. He could scarcely give clearer proof of his symbolic intention."[20]

> Oft have I seen, when break of day was nigh,
> The orient flushing with a rose-red gleam,
> The rest of heaven adorned with calm blue sky,
>
> Seen the sun's face rise shadowy and dim
> Through veils of mist, so tempering his powers,
> The eye might long endure to look on him;
>
> So even so, through cloud on cloud of flowers
> Flung from angelic hands and falling down
> Over the car and all around in showers,
>
> In a white veil beneath an olive-crown
> Appeared to me a lady cloaked in green,
> And living flame the colour of her gown;
>
> And instantly, for all the years between
> Since her mere presence with a kind of fright
> Could awe me and make my spirit faint within,
>
> There came on me, needing no further sight,
> Just by that strange, outflowing power of hers
> The old, old love in all its mastering might.
>   (XXX, 22–39)

He turns in his joy, as he has done for so long in his fears and pain, to his companion, his father, his friend,

> To say to Virgil: "There is scarce a dram
> That does not hammer and throb in all my blood;
> I know the embers of the ancient flame. . . ."
>   (XXX, 46–48)

What a tremendous assertion this is of the holiness of the flesh! His *whole* being recognizes his love.

> But Virgil—O he had left us, and we stood
> Orphaned of him; Virgil, dear father, most
> Kind Virgil I gave me to for my soul's good;

And not for all that our first mother lost
Could I forbid the smutching tears to steep
My cheeks. . . .

> (XXX, 49–54)

It is at this moment that Beatrice speaks—and her first word is Dante's name.

"Dante, weep not for Virgil's going—keep
As yet from weeping, weep not yet, for soon
Another sword shall give thee cause to weep."

> (XXX, 55–57)

And then, a little later,

"Look on us well; we are indeed, we are
Beatrice. How hast thou deigned to climb the hill?
Didst thou not know that man is happy here?"

> (XXX, 73–75)

It is the only time that Dante's name occurs in the *Commedia*. He apologizes for it, as a necessity here, since it was felt to be bad taste for a writer to mention his own name. The effect is therefore very great. Beatrice's first words, standing there on the car in her great symbolic role, are a clear and vehement assertion of his human identity and hers. She is in very truth Beatrice and he the boy she knew in Florence. Here and here alone in her speech with him she uses the royal "we"; and we cannot doubt the deliberate symbolism of this. When a royal person uses the plural "we," he conveys to his hearers that he is both himself and the carrier of an impersonal symbolic authority. He accepts the responsibility of his words both as *a* person and as *the* king. So Beatrice here, as she affirms her personal reality, reveals by that unexpected plural that she is also fully conscious of her impersonal identity, as God-bearing image—and that the second truth in no way destroys the first. It is an affirmation of the mystery of incarnation, and of personal immortality—"Guarda ci ben; ben sem, ben sem Beatrice"—in its context and its depth of meaning one of the greatest lines in the poem.

Between the "Dante" and the "Beatrice" of her first greeting lies a rebuke. Dante has come through the long purging; he stands on the threshold of innocence and joy where "all shall be well and all manner of thing shall be well," and he indulges in a fit of weeping over the necessary parting with Virgil.

"Dante, weep not for Virgil's going—keep
As yet from weeping, weep not yet, for soon
Another sword shall give thee cause to weep."
(XXX, 55–57)

She is even ironic.

". . . How has thou deigned to climb the holy hill?
Didst thou not know that man is happy here?"
(XXX, 74–75)

Even the heavenly beings who surround her are moved to pity and a feeling that she is over-stern, and certainly our first reaction is that she is indeed hard on his most natural and human reaction to such a separation. But if we look deeper, we begin to understand. She certainly is not rebuking him for his inevitable grief at the parting. We rightly feel suffering when we must leave behind a way of life or an attitude which has been up to this point an unqualified good; and when outwardly or inwardly we must part from those who have brought us to the new threshold and whom we have greatly loved. What is no longer allowed is the emotional indulgence of this suffering on a personal, self-pitying level. Tears indeed are still to come, tears of quite another kind which will finally submerge us in Lethe and Eunoe and bring us to established joy; but to weep long at this point for a personal loss could be a fatal evasion, a betrayal of the joy in the heart of the quest. It is in fact an evasion of a kind we all know—the refusal of the responsibility of joy and freedom on the threshold of a new awareness for which we have long striven. We very often deserve Beatrice's words. We condescend to climb and struggle, but we won't condescend to be happy.

Dante is now at the point where he must look back on his whole life and remember with absolute clarity and without any vestige of excuse-making every smallest betrayal of the vision which had been given him in his youth, and he must recognize such betrayal as the black thing that it is. Only in that final experience of contrition in which the ego is ground to powder will the split in the psyche be healed. "Only when the last lingering vestige of unconscious assent (to sin) has been purged away" in Dorothy Sayers' words, can the full realization of true guilt be borne. Before this point if a man were to see himself so clearly, he would be submerged in remorse and false guilt, and the final cleansing tears of total contrition would be impossible. At Peter's Gate, Dante had made an "act" of contrition; he had recognized its nature and had chosen to suffer the purging of his unconscious motives. Here, after the passage of the fire, the final knowledge of contrition comes to him. "All shall be well and all manner of thing shall be well/By the purification of the motive/In the ground of our beseeching" (T.S. Eliot quoting the Lady Julian, *Four Quartets*).

Dante's long journey down and up has brought him at last to look again clear-eyed on her whom he truly loved with his whole heart on earth, and she will lead him to the fullness of love in Heaven, but not before she has ruthlessly exposed to him his infidelities. She stresses the extraordinary gifts of nature and grace which were his and which enabled him when he fell in love in his youth to catch so clear a glimpse of the end in the beginning. His early poems, in the *Vita Nuova*, leave us in no doubt of the new life which his love opened in him; nor does Beatrice.

> Not the great wheels alone, whose workings tend,
> As in their aspects all their stars congress,
> To guide each seed to its appropriate end,
>
> But graces also of divine largesse,
> Which have their rains from clouds too high to see,
> They so transcend our eyesight's littleness,
>
> Had so endowed this man, potentially,
> In his new life, that from such gifts as those
> A wondrous harvest should have come to be.
>
> (XXX, 109–117)

I believe her reference here is not only to his new inner life but to his first book, *La Vita Nuova*, at the close of which he had written, "It was given to me to behold a wonderful vision, wherein I saw things which determined me to say nothing further of this blessed one (Beatrice) until such time as I could discourse more worthily concerning her. And to this end I labor all I can, as she in truth knoweth. Therefore, if it be His pleasure in whom is the life of all things, that my life continue with me a few years, it is my hope that I shall yet write concerning her what hath not before been written of any woman." The *Vita Nuova* was certainly written soon after Beatrice's death in 1290; Dante was exiled in 1302; and the first manuscript of the *Inferno* was circulating in 1314. What had been going on in the years between? He had written two quite different kinds of work, the philosophical *Convivio* and the politico-philosophical *De Monarchia*.

Thus Beatrice goes on to accuse Dante of having forsaken the truth his wholehearted devotion had taught him:

> "And by wild ways he wandered, seeking for
> False phantoms of the good, which promise make
> Of joy, but never fully pay the score.
>
> With inspirations, prayer-wrung for his sake,
> Vainly in dreams and other ways as well
> I called him home; so little did he reck.
>
> And, in the end, to such a depth he fell
> That every means to save his soul came short
> Except to let him see the lost in hell."
>
> (XXX, 130–138)

These words are spoken to the angelic beings who thought her too severe. Now she turns on Dante himself and demands from him a straight answer to her accusations:

> . . . "In that desire of me which bore
> Thy love along with it to seek the Good
> Past which there's nothing to be eager for,
>
> What didst thou find? what pitfalls in the road?
> What chains? that thou shouldst cast all hope away
> Of pressing onward as a traveller should?
>
> And what allurement, what advantage, pray,
> Seemed in those rival favours so to lie
> That thou must bow and scrape to such as they?"
>
> (XXXI, 22–30)

People have speculated as to what kind of infidelities were hinted at. As with all of us they must have been legion, and their details do not matter; but when a poet is in question, most of all a poet of Dante's stature, the major betrayal to which Beatrice refers must surely have been a turning away from the poetic vision of love to which he had pledged devotion in the last words of the *Vita Nuova*. There are certain signs in the *Convivio*, for instance, that Dante did just this. In her essay, "And Telling You a Story," Dorothy Sayers wrote, "The Dante of the *Convivio* has everything that the other Dante has—the great intellect, the great curiosity, the great poetry, the great piety, even—but without humility and without charity. The sin is not primarily girls or anybody's system of philosophy; it is simply the thing known as hardness of heart. . . ."[21] In the *Convivio*, as she points out, he was apt to lecture people, to tell his readers how he had matured since writing the *Vita Nuova*, to talk down to them. Then he tries to explain his obvious love poems in terms of philosophy and allegory, so that the immediacy of feeling, of love and pain and laughter, is turned to cold reason. When this happens to a man, he will, of course, at the same time be delivered over to sensuality. These are indeed the twin poles of hardness of heart—cold intellect and sensuality. It landed Dante in the dark wood, undermining and threatening his integrity as poet and man. He emerged, after the long journey, to write the *Commedia* in that abiding spirit of humility which brings true self-confidence. His charity shines through all one hundred cantos of his poem. He has entirely escaped from lecturing people; on the contrary, he makes the reader "his familiar friend," sharing with him his highest, his lowest, and his most ridiculous moments.

Beatrice's indictment is truly the same for all of us in our degree. If we have even once been capable of falling into a love which opens our hearts to that joy which excludes nothing in the universe, however little we understand it at the time, then, as soon as we return to partial goals, "seeking for false phantoms of the good," we are on the way to the dark wood of hardness of heart where we may or may not be saved by the memory of that love. The forms of our personal phantoms are infinitely varied—the betrayal is one, and if pursued to the end is the road to the frozen pit of Judecca. Partially recognized in the dark wood, this betrayal cannot be fully known and accepted until we are ready to look again, with as profound humility and love as did Dante, on the reality we have rejected.

Whose form will each of us see standing on the car, when we come to this moment? For the human Beatrice on *her* journey, it might have been Dante, or it might have been another—of either sex. For some there may be no doubt at all—the beloved's image may have been a life-long companion; but for others the shining memory may have been dimmed and hidden, to be reborn in the images rising from the unconscious in dream or imaginative vision.

It is a very common experience; everyone who has truly "fallen in love" has had it, and sex in the narrow sense is not the important thing. It is the recognition of "our native country" through love of another. We glimpse his or her eternal identity and so also our own, and we know in that moment that we have the freedom of that country forever. But we forget so quickly, "seeking false phantoms," and sometimes absolutely; or else we do worse and decry the vision as a romantic "nothing but." That is betrayal indeed.

There is a beautiful passage in C.S. Lewis' *Till We Have Faces* which exactly describes the Dantean experience of re-encounter at the end of the long and purging return. For Orual in the story, her sister Psyche was the love of her life through whom she had once glimpsed the reality of incarnation. That love had been tarnished firstly by the arguments of reason, then by possessiveness and jealousy leading to bitterness against God and man. Since her loss of Psyche she had rejected all joy and suffered horribly through the years of her long life; but she had taken up all her responsibilities without complaint and had endured her purgatory. Then at the end she comes in a vision to her judgment; and, as Dante did, she finally sees her so-called devotion for the partial, self-regarding thing it had become. All her excuses, her complaints against the gods are over. She is in the state of complete contrition—like Dante, she falls into nothingness, and then meets Psyche again, Psyche redeemed and whole. "Now I knew that she was a goddess indeed—and yet— with all this, even because of all this, she was the old Psyche still, a thousand times more her very self than she had been before" the parting. "For all that had then but flashed out in a glance or a gesture, all that one meant most when one spoke her name, was now wholly present, not to be gathered up from hints nor in shreds, not some of it in one moment and some in another. Goddess? I had never seen a real woman before."[22] Beatrice expresses all this in that one line spoken from the holy car: "Guarda ci ben; ben sem, ben sem Beatrice." In very truth she is Beatrice, but she is also Dante's "Psyche," his own innermost reality.

Dante, choked by tears, has spoken clearly and without excuse his assent to Beatrice's words, but his head is bent in

shame and he has not yet truly looked at her. Beatrice, therefore, tells him that it is time to abandon his childish shame, "to
lift up his beard" and look. He obeys and looks unsteadily
across the stream at Beatrice, and sees that *her* gaze is turned
away from him towards the Gryphon, and is fixed on that
symbol of "him that is one person sole in natures two." At this
sight his grief at his betrayals becomes so overwhelming that
he falls in a faint. When he comes to himself, he is aware of
Matilda bending over him.

> I saw my first-met, lone-met lady bent
> Above me, saying: "Hold on, hold on to me."
>
> Into the stream she'd drawn me in my faint,
> Throat-high, and now, towing me after her,
> Light as a shuttle o'er the water went.
> . . . .
>
> She stretched both hands, she seized me by the crown,
> Did that fair lady, and she plunged me in,
> So that I needs must drink the water down;
>
> Then drew me forth and led me, washed and clean,
> Within the dance. . . .
>
> (XXXI, 92–104)

Matilda's *function* as a forerunner of Beatrice is here very
plainly the same as St. John the Baptist's as forerunner of
Christ, but in her personal aspect she is about as different as
can be imagined. Here is another unmistakable affirmation of
the individual nature of our experience of the way. For Dante
it was no dour ascetic who submerged him in the waters of his
new baptism, washing away his sin. For every man the forerunner is unique, as the sacramental image is unique.

We may perhaps come to moments of overwhelming clarity
about our shadow selves, but we remain with our heads bent,
caught by remorse; and then we seek release by some act of
will or through some lesser light. We do not dare, we are not
yet able, simply to lift our eyes and look across the stream in
full acceptance of the fact that the one we most love and who
is also our own inmost psyche has eternally turned away from
every small ego-concern, and gazes on the Self, the Christ.
This was the thing that Orual could not do until the end of
Lewis' story. She was furiously angry when she realized that

Fig. 32: The Earthly Paradise; immersion in Lethe

Psyche no longer put her sister's love first, that she was now wholly obedient to the God and derived her joy from him. Orual thereafter projected her bitter anger onto the gods themselves. When once we are humble enough to look clearly on the beloved, the psyche itself, and see that she gazes forever at the Self, then the ego as the *center* of our lives will receive its mortal blow; it will become nothing, be unmade, as Orual puts it, and so we shall be born anew out of the water.

With Dante, as with Orual, it was fidelity in his outer life (symbolized by Matilda as it was also symbolized by St. John the Baptist), the acceptance of its responsibilities, its conflicts and simplicities, that carried him finally into the cleansing stream so that he needs must drink, and led him out again into the dance around the car. And now he stands before Beatrice without fear or guilt and looks into her eyes as they gaze upon the Gryphon ("the orbs of emerald whence Love let fly his further shafts").

Once more the memory of his young love is evoked side by side with the present splendor.

> Myriad desires, hotter than fire or scald
> Fastened mine eyes upon the shining eyes
> That from the Gryphon never loosed their hold,

Like sun in looking-glass, no otherwise,
I saw the Twyform mirrored in their range,
Now in the one, now in the other guise.

Think, Reader, think how marvellous and strange
It seemed to me when I beheld the thing
Itself stand changeless and the image change.

(XXXI, 118–126)

All desires have become one. His gaze is fixed on her eyes, and in them is reflected the incarnation of Love. Dante sees the image, now as wholly divine, now as wholly human. He knows that the two natures are one simultaneous reality, but cannot as yet see the unchanging One except in the allegorical figure of the Gryphon; for the direct vision he must wait until he has reached the center of Paradise. First must come long devotion to the reflected image in Beatrice's eyes and an ever deepening experience of joy in the spheres of Heaven.

Beatrice, urged by the three dancing maidens, Faith, Hope, and Charity, unveils to Dante not only her eyes but her mouth. From now on until the end, Beatrice's eyes and Beatrice's smile are the lodestars of his journey, increasing in radiance and unclouded beauty from sphere to sphere. In the *Convivio* he wrote, "What is a smile but the coruscation of the joy of the soul, like the outward shining of an inward light." As he looks for the first time upon it after ten years, he is dazzled and has to be brought back to awareness of the "lesser lights" of the procession, which is moving again, wheeling round from Lethe and passing through the Forest. Dante, Matilda, and Statius walk on the left of the car. They come to a huge barren tree in the midst of the green wood, the Tree of Knowledge; and here Beatrice descends from the car and the Gryphon binds the pole of the chariot, which is the image of the Cross, to its trunk.

The allegory is obvious; immediately every branch of the vast tree bursts into leaf and flower, and the voices of all the actors are lifted in a song so sweet that Dante is lulled to sleep. When he awakes, the Gryphon and all the others have gone, except Matilda, Statius, and the seven nymphs who surround Beatrice, sitting on a root of the tree. There follows a second allegorical masque in which the history of the corruption of the Church since the Resurrection is shown forth. Briefly, the tree is stripped of its blossoms again, the car of the Church is defiled, turns into the Beast of the Apocalypse, and upon it sit a harlot and a giant embracing and kissing. The harlot casts flirting glances on Dante, whereupon the giant in a fury drags her and the beast away into the Forest. The masque is over.

The allegory of the giant and the harlot is concerned with the split in the Papacy in the early fourteenth century, when a rival pope set up his court in Avignon. Symbolically, it is a warning of what happens when our deepest commitment is invaded and split by the power drives and concupiscence of the ego. Giant and harlot, cold brutality and indiscriminate sensuality, are now in control of the great four-wheeled chariot which is the image of incarnate wholeness.

The pageant is over, and Beatrice with her company leads Dante towards the spring from which Lethe and Eunoe flow. As they go, she instructs Dante on the meaning of what he has seen and urges him to write it down when he returns to earth; but, seeing that his mind is bewildered, almost numbed, by her explanation, she says:

> "But since I see thy mind is turned to stone,
> And dull as stone, so that it is not lit
> By my words' light, but dazzled and outdone,
>
> In heart I'd have thee bear them—if not writ,
> Then at least pictured. . . ."
>
> (XXXIII, 73–77)

Thus Dante once more asserts the power of the image by which we recognize and remember and feel in our heart the unknown realities when we cannot yet be fully aware of them.

We have come almost to the end of the *Purgatorio*, and here Dante's genius brings to us, after the complicated drama of the masque and as a prelude to the high and holy moment of his final passage of the water, an incident of simple human gaiety. Standing before the twin fountain of Lethe and Eunoe, Dante asks, "What water's this?" whereupon Matilda and Beatrice indulge in a little affectionate teasing. Matilda reminds him that she has already told him all about it and adds that Lethe cannot be held responsible for his lapse of memory since it was surely not sinful knowledge. Beatrice adds that he must have had other things on his mind—meaning obviously his preoccupation with her! What other poet could have done such a thing at this point without a disastrous break in the feeling

Fig. 33: The Earthly Paradise; Eunoe

tone? But since Dante's deep seriousness is never tainted by
a portentous solemnity, is never separated from true human
feeling, his gaiety is therefore never frivolous or jarring; indeed
it not only enhances the depth of his vision, it is an essential
part of it.

Matilda takes Dante by the hand, "Saying in tones of wom-
anly sweet grace to Statius, 'Come with him'; and so led on."
As he enters the waters of Eunoe and drinks deep of the sweet
water, the memory of darkness and sin is restored to him, but
this time cleansed of all shame, fully present and redeemed.
At the passage of Lethe forgiveness is freely given, and at that
first moment of relief it may be that we put all the dark things
away and feel as though they had never been, returning for a
brief space to the unconscious innocence of Eden. Indeed, we
may recognize this tendency in moments when we feel forgiven by another and imagine that this wipes out the fault and

that we may forget it. But it would be deadly to stay long in this frame of mind. Forgiveness must be accepted as well as given, the whole responsibility for every betrayal taken up, before it can become "a happy fault" which has taken its place as an essential part of man's completeness.

> From those most holy waters, born anew
> I came, like trees by change of calendars
> Renewed with new-sprung foliage through and through,
>
> Pure and prepared to leap up to the stars.

> Io ritornai da la santissima onda
> rifatto sì come piante novelle
> rinovellate di novella fronda,
>
> puro e disposto a salire a le stelle.
>> (XXXIII, 142–145)

The Paradiso

Introduction

PART I

> The glory of Him who moves all things soe'er
> Impenetrates the universe, and bright
> The splendour burns, more here and lesser there.
>
> Within that heav'n which most receives His light
> Was I, and saw such things as man nor knows
> Nor skills to tell, returning from that height;
>
> For when our intellect is drawing close
> To its desire, its paths are so profound
> That memory cannot follow where it goes.
>
> Yet now, of that blest realm whate'er is found
> Here in my mind still treasured and possessed
> Must set the strain for all my song to sound.
>
> Gracious Apollo! in the crowning test
> Make me the conduit that thy power runs through!
>
> . . . .
>
> Breathe in me, breathe, and from my bosom drive
> Music like thine. . . .
>
> O power divine, grant me in song to show
> The blest realm's image—shadow though it be—
> Stamped on my brain. . . .
>
> > (I, 1–24)

Some people have maintained that while Dante achieved a very great imaginative foretaste of what the ultimate state of bliss might be like, yet there is no proof that he did in fact experience the reality of the vision for which the whole of the *Commedia* is a preparation. I find it unbelievable that he could have written the opening words of the *Paradiso* quoted above, still less the final canto itself, unless he had, however briefly, passed consciously beyond all images to that inexpressible realization.

Dante tells us from the beginning that the state of bliss is *one* and that all the souls to whom he speaks dwell equally at the center, "within that Heaven which is God's quietude" (II, 112). They are shown to him, however, as a hierarchy, in lesser and greater images, because he is, in the story, as yet incapable of apprehending that unity which contains all diversity and is beyond time and space. The structure of Paradise is based on the cosmology of the day, and different souls appear to him on each of the seven planets and in the realm of the fixed stars. He then enters the sphere of the angels and comes at last to the Empyrean and the white rose of the center where he experiences the final unity. So "in song" he shows us the "blest realm's image—shadow though it be."

Dorothy Sayers died in 1957, having completed the translation of twenty cantos of the *Paradiso*. Barbara Reynolds, who had been her friend and very close to her throughout her work on Dante, admirably completed the translation and wrote the introduction and notes. She makes a most interesting comparison between the thought and imagery of Teilhard de Chardin and Dante and says that, in many ways, our vastly expanded knowledge of the universe would have been an easier framework than the concepts of his own time for Dante's symbolism. Let no one then be put off by the intricacies of medieval cosmology and philosophy. Dante used the language of his time, as we all must, to communicate the eternal truth that, as Barbara Reynolds puts it, "Each consciousness exists for ever as itself, but can only be fully realized as itself by integration with the Whole. . . ." She adds that the more clearly distinct from others a person becomes, the closer he is to the All. "In both Dante and Teilhard the relationship of the Many to the One is perceived as the persistence of the personal consciousness (i.e. the soul) and the centring of the consciousness upon the centre of all centres (i.e., God)."[23] Earlier, in her introduction, she says, "It is in the *Paradiso* that we find affirmed with the utmost clarity and consistency the fundamental Christian proposition that the journey to God is the journey into reality. To know all things in God is to know them as they really are. . . . When Dante and his poem venture . . . into the world of Reality, his guide is Beatrice, who represents his own personal experience of the immanence of the Creator in the creature. In her he had seen, in those moments of revelation which he describes in the *Vita Nuova*, the eternal Beauty shining through the created beauty, the reality of Beatrice as God knew her."[24]

This then is what the *Paradiso* is about—the relationship of the unique person to the whole, and the final unity of time and eternity which is bliss. Many poets have touched this theme in words and images; indeed the intuition of this truth is the creative power at the heart of all great art. Dante alone, however, has dared to take us into this realm of joy and keep us there for thirty-three cantos, calling upon us to exercise every faculty of our being to the uttermost, so that, if we once give ourselves up to his meaning, we can never again imagine Heaven as a bodiless spirituality, a vague emotional ecstasy, or a dissolution into nothingness.

For Dante, the whole is not an undifferentiated concept or an indefinite blaze of light; it is literally everything. If it is to be known, it must come to us simultaneously through clarity and precision of thought, through intensity and subtlety of feeling, through the unclouded perception of the senses, and through the intuitive vision which unites them all. All these things his poetry awakens in us through images—from the most homely and everyday to the most sublime—images of sight and sound, of movement and color, and, above all, of light which is both single and patterned in infinite variety. "Nowhere in poetry has experience so remote from ordinary experience been expressed so concretely, by a masterly use of that image of light. . ." writes T.S. Eliot. He also says, "Once we have got the hang of the kind of feeling in it [the *Paradiso*], no one part of it is difficult. . . . the *Paradiso* is never dry, it is either incomprehensible or intensely exciting."[25] For we are listening not only to some of the most glorious poetry ever written, but to a *story*—the story of an ordinary flesh-and-blood man like ourselves, whose experience of human love grows and expands into divinity, deepens and contracts to a single point, so that his whole being is drawn as by a magnet to the vision of God. This is not the experience of an ascetic set apart in a realm we cannot hope to reach; we have only to follow our own human love to its root, to come at the last to that same great vision.

Nevertheless there has been a widespread belief that whereas the *Inferno* and the *Purgatorio* may speak to the mind and heart of the ordinary reader, the *Paradiso* is something to be left to the scholars; for surely nobody but an expert could want to struggle with the outdated views of the cosmos and the "dry" scholastic philosophy to be found there, or listen to lengthy descriptions of joy and bliss which must, it is assumed, be boring. It is a strange thing that most people are convinced that descriptions of bliss must be dull. It is probably because joy is confused with a superficial optimism, with that cheeriness which is, as Eliot says, much farther from joy than Hell itself. Thus many people who have loved the first two Canticas do not even start on the third. For this, the fact that many of the commentators have indeed been scholars without true poetic insight has been responsible. They do, of course, point out that the poetry in the *Paradiso* is even more beautiful than in the other Canticas in spite of the subject matter—which is surely nonsense. Style in a supremely great poet is not something which can be separated from his matter; if the poetry rises to new heights of beauty and power, we may be sure the subject does too.

The opening lines of the second canto are addressed specifically to his readers, and Dante seems to have had a clear intuition of what his future critics would say. It would seem that he agrees with them that the *Paradiso* is not for the many, but for opposite reasons. Those he warns off are precisely those readers who approach it with a superficial scholarly or aesthetic attitude. He tells us ruthlessly that it would be better not to read the *Paradiso* at all than to read it simply because we have enjoyed his poetry so far and want to hear some more. That attitude has been allowable in the other two realms but will no longer serve.

> O you that follow in light cockle-shells,
> For the song's sake, my ship that sails before,
> Carving her course and singing as she sails,
>
> Turn back and seek the safety of the shore;
> Tempt not the deep, lest, losing unawares
> Me and yourselves, you come to port no more.
>
> (II, 1–6)

It is a severe warning indeed. Easily enough we pass over it, half-consciously assuming it to be a beautiful poetic exaggeration, not meant to be taken literally. Yet, if we have learnt anything about Dante from the first two Canticas we know that he never indulges in hyperbole or succumbs to vagueness, and that every word he utters he passionately means. We are warned, then, that to follow Dante through Paradise with wrong or inadequate motives is not only fruitless but dangerous. If we try to explore these deep seas of being, either in a spirit of dry theory or in an emotional, starry-eyed way, we shall not only miss Dante's meaning, but lose touch with our own inner guide, and finally be swamped ourselves by the negative side of the "deep" we have "tempted." Jung often issued the same warning. It is better not to start on the way of individuation at all than to turn back halfway, for that can spell disaster.

Dante, however, goes on to say that there are a few who may safely follow and what it is that distinguishes these few:

> But you, rare souls, that have reached up to seize
> Betimes the bread of angels, food for men
> To live on here, whereof no surfeit is,
>
> You may commit your bark unto the main,
> Hard on my keel, where ridge and furrow flee
> Ere the vext waters level out again.
>> (II, 10–15)

The condition is clear: those few may dare to sail with him who have recognized that the "bread of angels" is not something remote or theoretical but is the food which sustains us here and now in this life in every moment, and of which no man can ever have too much. Moreover they must keep so close to Dante's ship as to sail in the furrow made by his keel—which must mean that a tremendous effort of close attention and of the imagination is necessary if we are to stay with him to the end. The thirst for the "god-like realm," which is innate in every soul, however tragically misunderstood and misdirected, will then draw us swiftly in his wake. We may well quail at this passage, thinking to be humble; and, since we feel certain that we are not one of the "rare souls," we are tempted to turn back. The condition, however, is not one of merit; we do not have to have achieved some high vision in order to follow safely; we have only to recognize and give ourselves up to that which is born in all of us, the longing for wholeness, and, in a literal translation, "straighten our necks to receive the bread of angels." It gives one the feeling of simply having to stand erect and look straight and without evasion at whatever is before us, light or dark, good or evil, in order to be fed here on earth by the bread of heaven, whereby the two worlds will ultimately be known as one. That we are unlikely to reach this wholeness here in this world does not matter, so long as we never look back, once we have launched our bark and are ready to sail before the winds of God in the wake of the inner guide.

PART II

We have now to "get the hang of the kind of feeling" in the *Paradiso*, to use Eliot's phrase. Here, for instance, the "gateways" from one level to another are no longer a matter of climbing down or up, of overcoming obstacles or passing through fire and water. If we are to follow Dante in this high realm, we must feel and think with him in a new way; and the stages of the journey are marked simply by the deepening intensity of this feeling and of the urge to understand. "From one small spark springs up a mighty flare; if I set forth, others may come behind," says Dante. This spark is lit in the first two cantos, where at the outset the feeling tone of the *Paradiso* is set; and thereafter it burns more and more brilliantly until it blazes out in the great mysteries of the end. We, though we do not yet see with unclouded vision, may nevertheless catch the spark through our yearning for the bread of angels and, following with the expanding strength of our imagination, may at least glimpse the reflected light of the glory.

The *Paradiso* is a supreme flowering of the "feeling intellect" (Wordsworth). Dante assumes that any reader who loves as he loves will also be consumed with the longing for precise knowledge. For him, it is plainly inconceivable that any intense emotion should remain an undefined ecstasy; always his feeling experiences are accompanied by an all-out effort of his mind to understand. Indeed it may be said that true feeling is born precisely when this effort is made to discriminate and to define the meaning of an emotion without destroying it. Conversely, thought is never creative in the true sense until it is infused with feeling, with the values of the heart.

Dante stood on the threshold of the Renaissance and of the modern world in which the individual consciousness would gradually break all the bounds of tradition and external authority and dare to challenge every assumption of the medieval mind. He stood there, rooted in the certainties of his time, yet pointing the way, singing the praises of doubt as the only means of knowledge. His terminology is alien to most of us, his factual knowledge of the universe puerile in our eyes, yet across the centuries his penetration to the essential truths remains. For he was a supreme poet and therefore affirms with incomparable power the unchanging psychic realities behind all the changing beliefs and rebellions of mankind. He speaks to the poet hidden in each of us, without whom all our specialized knowledge and our passionate devotions are so much chaff. He thus addresses Beatrice:

"O loved," said I, "of the First Lover! O
Most heavenly Lady, by whose words I live
More and yet more, bathed in their quickening glow,
. . . .

That nothing save the light of truth allays
Our intellect's disquiet I now see plain—
God's truth, which holds all truth within its rays.

Intellect, like a wild thing in its den,
When it has run and reached it, there can rest,
As reach it must, else all desire were vain.

Hence, at the foot of truth, the undying quest
Springs like a shoot, and doubt is still the lure
That speeds us toward the height from crest to crest."

(IV, 118–132)

And Beatrice replies:

"If in the fire of love I flame thus hot
Upon thee, past all wont or mortal mood,
Forcing thine eyes' surrender, marvel not;

This comes of perfect sight, with power endued
To apprehend, and foot by foot to move
Deeper into the apprehended good.

Full well I see thine intellect give off
Splendours already of the eternal light
Which once to look upon is aye to love."

(V, 1–9)

This passage indeed conveys to us the atmosphere of the *Paradiso*. The movement in Heaven is from passionate vision to precise definition and back; and the whole is woven together, not only by the imagery of light, color, song, and dance, but by the vivid personal encounters with individual human souls, each with his or her eternal identity, each with his own unique relationship to the small, the particular, and the finite. All of these know because they love and love because they know. Through it all there sounds in our ears, in our minds and hearts, the tremendous music of the verse— the poetry that creates all these things and is created by them. So, as we read, for us also it may be that "the undying quest springs like a shoot" from the soil of doubt and love and the yearning for wholeness.

The Moon

THE ACTION OF the Cantica begins as Dante stands alone with Beatrice in the Earthly Paradise and sees her turn left and look up to gaze at the sun. Literally translated, Dante writes, "So from her act, poured through the eyes into my imagination, my own action took shape." It is a perfect description of the workings of the creative imagination—the act giving birth to the image and the image to conscious action and creation. Without the *imaginative* response, Dante's act would have been unproductive imitation; with it he follows, but the act is his own. In youth especially we are apt to think of all "following," or acceptance of another's point of view, as subservience. On the contrary, those people who announce with pride that they cannot work *under* anybody are in fact exposing their failure to emerge from adolescence. It is essential to be able to follow those whom we respect if we are ever to learn how to lead; but the nature of our following is of vital importance. It may indeed be blind subservience; and one could write pages in an effort to define the difference between this and free consent, without improving on those two brief lines of Dante's.

"So from her act, poured through the eyes into my imagination, my own action took shape." Dante is enabled through this kind of following to look for one brief moment straight at the noonday sun whose light no mortal eye can stand, and in that instant he sees a second sun, as it were, "a day within a day," shedding its light around him; and, as he looks back at Beatrice, he feels himself "transhumanized," and he adds that this thing cannot be described, only experienced.

The "day within the day" is a first glimmering of the full awareness of the Incarnation which is to come. He has a feeling of being in two dimensions at once, physical and spiritual, human and divine (not one after the other as when he looked at the Gryphon in the Earthly Paradise), and finds that he has been lifted up by the light itself both inwardly and literally.

He is shaken and bewildered by this unfamiliar kind of motion, but Beatrice turns to him and tells him to be rid of "false imagining" which only makes him dense. The *true* impact of the image had "transhumanized" him, but as yet he has not realized the new simplicity and is in danger of falling back into imagining complicated reasons for what is going on. This is a very familiar process in all of us who, after an immediate response to a great image, retreat into cause and effect reasoning and often kill the image by an anxious splitting of hairs.

Beatrice explains to Dante that every created being is drawn as by an irresistible magnet to its center as soon as all hindrances (the obstructions of unconscious refusal) have been swept away—a statement which carries the same truth as is insisted upon by the Indian sages who say that enlightenment comes through *remembering* our true identity, stripped of illusion. Thus the new mode of travel

> "Ought no more to surprise thee than to see
> A stream rush down from mountain crest to foot;
>
> Nay, but if thou, from every hindrance free,
> Shouldst hug the ground, that *would* be a surprise—
> As stillness in quick flame on earth would be."
>
> (I, 137–141)

Here all striving is at an end. We have to "get the hang" of that; strenuous "imaginings" give way to the free interplay of image and fact.

> That which is born with us and cannot die,
> Thirst for the godlike realm, had made us skirr
> Almost as swiftly as the visible sky.
>
> Beatrice gazed on heav'n and I on her. . . .
>
> (II, 19–22)

We may profitably note here that Dante would have moved not at all if he had insisted on continuing to gaze directly at Heaven instead of on his "god-bearing image." The prevalence of this fatal mistake is obvious—a mistake which leads to a false spirituality disconnected from the small happenings of our lives, as we attempt to find shortcuts to enlightenment.

Dante and Beatrice, having traveled at almost the speed of light, now arrive in the first heaven of the Moon.

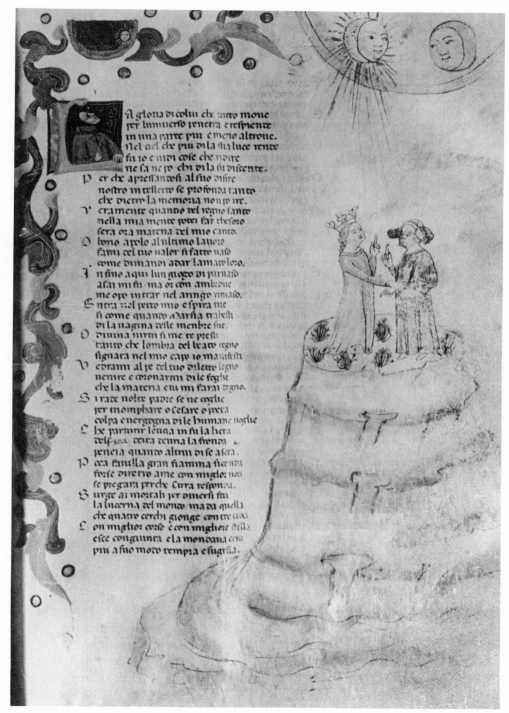

A gloria di colui che tutto move
per l'univerſo penetra e riſpiende
in una parte piu e meno altroue.
Nel ciel che piu dila ſua luce prende
fu io e uidi coſe che noire
ne ſa ne po chi dila ſu diſcende.

Per che apreſſandoſi al ſuo diſire
noſtro intelletto ſe profonda tanto
che dietro la memoria non po ire.

V eramente quanto del regno ſanto
nella mia mente potei far theſoro
ſera ora materia del mio canto.

O bono apolo al ultimo lauoro
fami del tuo ualor ſi fatto uaſo
come dimandi adar l'amato loro.

J nſino a qui lun giogo di parnaſo
aſai miſu ma or con ambedue
me opo intrar nel aringo rimaſo.

E ntra nel petto mio eſpira tue
ſi come quando marſia trabeſti
dila uagina delle membre ſue.

O diuina uirtu ſi me te preſti
tanto che lombra del beato regno
ſignata nel mio capo io manifeſti.

V edrami al pe del tuo diletto legno
nenire e coronarmi dile foghe
che la materia e tu mi farai regno.

S i rade uolte padre ſe ne coglie
per triomphar o ceſare o poeta
colpa e uergogna dile humane uoglie.

C he partirir letiaa in ſu la lieta
delfica deita douria la fronde
peneia quanto altrui diſe aſcia.

P oca ſauilla gran fiamma ſcurda
forſe direrio ame con miglo uoci
ſe pregam perche Cirra reſponda.

S urge ai mortali per diuerſi foci
la lucerna del mondo ma da quella
che quatro cerchi giongre con tre cruci

C on miglior corſo e con migliee ſtella
eſce congiunta ela mondana cera
piu aſuo moto tempra eſugella.

Fig. 34: *The ascent from the Earthly Paradise*

Fig. 35: Heaven of the Moon

Meseemed a cloud enclosed us, lucid, dense,
Solid, and smooth, like to the diamond stone
Smitten upon by the sun's radiance.

Into itself the eternal union
Received us both, as water doth receive
A ray of light and still remains all one.

(II, 31–36)

The word "union" is an ancient name for a single pearl, and is used here most aptly by Dorothy Sayers. The juxtaposition of the images of the reflected brilliance of the diamond and the opaque, cloud-like density of the pearl evoke an extraordinarily vivid feeling of the beauty of the moon, its brilliant light and its solid texture. Dante enters the "pearl," and the pearl remains uncleft. We on this earth cannot conceive, says the poet, how one body can enter another and each can be at the same time separate and one; all the more then must we yearn to see that

Essence wherein we behold how our own nature and God's
are one.

> What faith holds here shall there be known by seeing;
> Not demonstrated, but self-evident
> Like those prime truths that brook no disagreeing.
>   (II, 43–46)

So, once more, here at the beginning Dante evokes our intuition of the end. The stages of his ascent through the heavens are successive manifestations in relative terms of the essence which is one and whole; and it is through these manifestations that his capacity to bear the full light is gradually strengthened. He is made aware of this expansion of consciousness through the ever-increasing joy which shines in his eyes and in the smile of Beatrice. It is as though we are constantly reminded that all the great visions which Dante sees on his own through the heavens are made real, incarnate, for him by his unwavering attention to the image of his human love as it grows closer to "the love which moves the Sun and the other stars."

It is in the lowest heaven of the Moon that Beatrice expounds to Dante, in the first of the great discourses of the *Paradiso*, the nature of the paradox to which I have referred. Exteriorly she explains the differences in the apparent density of the moon; inwardly she uses this image to demonstrate how all the souls in Paradise dwell in the perfect bliss of the center while there is yet a hierarchy and a diversity. There, as here on earth, equality of value, of essence, does not imply a sameness of capacity. The individual remains distinct as much by what he is not as by what he is. Beatrice's words are an approach, as explicit as was possible at that time, to the same truth that Jung affirmed when he said that the goal of individuation was completeness, not perfection.

Dante is now ready to encounter individuals in the first three heavens who will make real for him the words of Beatrice. The souls whom he meets in the Moon are those who, when faced with pressure and threat, were not wholly faithful to their religious vows. In the next heaven of Mercury are the people who, having great gifts of leadership, had assumed heavy responsibilities in the world, and carried them out with integrity; but, mixed with their selflessness, there had been a certain pride and joy in their own achievements. The planet Venus is the realm of those with a natural gift for loving who overindulged this gift. They were filled with generous and affectionate ardor but nevertheless were blinded by this to other values. Through these meetings we are reminded of the passage of the stream Eunoe at the end of the *Purgatorio* and what it meant. A man's sins are not left behind on the threshold of Heaven. In their redeemed state—that is, when the conscious responsibility for them has been fully accepted and suffered, as in Dante's terrible moment beside Lethe—they become themselves a matter of joy, an essential part of a man's wholeness.

As he stands now in the cloudy brightness of the moon, Dante sees faces like reflections in clear water, or, he says in a beautiful image, like a pearl faintly stirring on a white forehead; and, thinking that they are indeed reflections, he turns round hoping to see their actuality. But Beatrice smiles and tells him that what he took for reflection is true substance. So indeed do we tend to refuse substance to our first dim glimpses of a new dimension of being.

At this point I struggled to summarize Dante's conversation with Piccarda dei Donati (the sister of Dante's Florentine friend, Forese dei Donati), but I could not do it as I turned back to the great beauty of the actual words. It is so lovely a passage and so vital to the theme of the nature of bliss as completeness, that I will quote the greater part of it. Moreover, reading it, we feel Dante's extraordinary power to convey his vision through a warm human meeting with a woman whose unique personality breathes life into the profundities of which she speaks.

> So, to the shade that seemed most keenly bent
> On speech, I now addressed myself, although
> Over-excitement made me diffident:
>
> "Soul made for bliss, enjoying in the glow
> Of life eternal those sweet mysteries
> Which, till they're tasted, pass man's wit to know,
>
> If it so please thee, I should dearly prize
> Some news of you—your status, and thy name."
> And she replied at once with dancing eyes:
>
> "Our love would no more turn a rightful claim
> Back from the door, than His who is indeed
> Love's self, and will have all His court the same.

On earth I was a nun; my present meed
Of greater beauty should not cloud thy view;
If thou but search thy memory with good heed

Surely my name will come to thee anew—
Piccarda, that with all this blessed host
Joined in the slowest sphere, am blessed too.

The sole good-pleasure of the Holy Ghost
Kindles our hearts, which joyously espouse,
Informed by Him, whate'er delights Him most.

This lot, which seems but as a lowly house,
Is given to us because we did withal
Neglect and partly disavow our vows."

Then I to her: "The features I recall
Are changed by something of a wondrous kind—
Some divine likeness mirrored in you all;

This made my recognition lag behind;
Now that thy words have helped to make things clear
I bring thy face more readily to mind.

But tell me, you whose happiness is here,
Have you no hankering to go up higher,
To win more insight or a love more dear?"

She smiled a little, and the spirit-choir
Smiled too; and when she spoke her looks expressed
Such joy, she seemed to burn in love's first fire:

"Brother, our love has laid our wills to rest,
Making us long only for what is ours,
And by no other thirst to be possessed.

. . . .

Nay, 'tis the essence of our blissful fate
To dwell in the divine will's radius,
Wherein our wills themselves are integrate;

Whose being from threshold unto threshold thus
Through all this realm doth all the realm so please,
And please the King that here in-willeth us

To His own will; and His will is our peace;
This is the sea whereunto all things fare
That it creates or nature furnishes."

                    (III, 34–87)

"*E sua voluntade è nostra pace.*" It is another of the most quoted of Dante's sayings, but in its context it is immensely more powerful than most people who know the words realize. The three lines literally translated are: "And His will is our peace; it is that sea to which all moves that it creates or nature makes." The image of the sea, the mother of all life on earth, is here a symbol of the end as it is of the beginning. The highest consciousness of man and all things, down to the first cell of living matter and beyond to the mysterious constituents of the atom, were created by and return to the "sea" which is eternally both His will and our peace. This conscious return is the *hierosgamos* of matter and spirit, of humanity and the Godhead, for "all creation is feminine to God" (Origen); and the passage is a forerunner of that great line with which Dante opens the last canto of his poem: "*Vergine Madre, figlia del tuo figlio*" ("Virgin Mother, daughter of your son").

An alternative reading accepted by some is "*En sua voluntade è nostra pace*"—"*in* His will is our peace." The difference is considerable, and Dante being Dante, I think we may be sure that the reading "*E sua voluntade,*" "*and* His will is our peace," is the correct one. We do not simply derive our peace from following what we conceive to be the will of God; His will and our peace are literally one thing. There is no peace for man which is not in its essence the affirmation that every fact is our will as well as His; and His will is impotent in the psyche (through which comes our awareness of any level of reality) without the peace born of a man's conscious sacrifice of the ego's hubris.

It follows that it is only out of this fundamental serenity beyond the warring opposites that any truly creative work or act or thought or feeling is born. Other kinds of activity, from world-shaking revolutions to our smallest daily movements, do not create; they merely repeat the restless swing between one opposite and another, the good on one level balanced always by evil on another. It seems absurd to speak of serenity as the condition of creation, since we know that creativity is born of passion, tension, and conflict. The answer is that true peace excludes none of these things; indeed it is born of them. In Christ, in the Buddha, this truth is obvious; but if on another level nearer our own we think of some of the unquestionably great creators of the world's history whom we all know and recognize, we will realize that it still holds, since we cannot doubt for a moment that their work sprang out of an underlying deep peace of spirit—"the still point of the turning world" (T.S. Eliot). Their themes may express the extremes of evil and unrest, their temperaments and their personal lives may have been turbulent and far from serene, but Shakespeare and Homer, for instance, could never have written the undying poetry in which they plumb the depths of evil and violence, as in *Macbeth*, *King Lear*, or the *Iliad*, unless, beyond these things, they had recognized the peace which passeth understanding and which Dante defined as "that sea to which all moves."

I am reminded here of the words of the alchemist, John Gower, which Jung used as a motto for the introduction to his work, *The Psychology of the Transference*: "*Bellica pax, vulnus dulce, suave malum*"—"A warring peace, a sweet wound, an agreeable evil." Jung comments, "Into these words the old alchemist put the quintessence of his experience. I can add nothing to their incomparable simplicity and conciseness. They . . . illuminate for [the ego] the paradoxical darkness of human life. Submission to the fundamental contrariety of human nature amounts to an acceptance of the fact that the psyche is at cross purposes with itself."[26] Only out of this paradox does the peace dawn, out of which, beyond "I want" or "I do not want," there springs a new birth, a true creation, in great things or in small.

So, reading these words of Dante, we have a glimmering perhaps of the Zen poet's meaning when he wrote of the sage sitting in deep peace beside a flowing stream and saying, "I command the stream to flow."

It is interesting to notice which phrases from great writers are passed from mouth to mouth and remembered by those who never read the original. Usually it is because people unconsciously recognize a fundamental truth of the psyche without thinking it out at all. "His will is our peace" is not just a pious motto, nor does it speak only to the saint or the great sage. In its context it is a touchstone whereby we may know the extent to which we are truly creators in our daily round of ordinary work and human contacts; and it may well transform our attitude when we realize that we may be aware of that peace precisely at those moments when the psyche is most acutely and miserably at cross purposes with itself.

The next canto contains Dante's puzzled questioning after this, his first encounter in Heaven, and Beatrice's answers.

He cannot see why Piccarda and the others were less than perfect, since they were *forced* to break their vows. Beatrice points out that a man may always choose to die rather than break a vow, but proceeds to define the nature of vows. The vow made to God may under no circumstances ever be broken without deadly sin, but the vow to a particular way of life may be broken if both "the golden key and the silver" unlock the door.

We discussed the meaning of these keys in the chapter on Peter's Gate. The vital truth for us here is the relevance of Beatrice's words to every man's commitments. If we set foot consciously on the way to individuation, we are wholly and totally committed, to the death, if need be. The outer forms of our lives, the work, the relationships which are the vehicles of this commitment, not only may but must be changed when they no longer serve the fundamental leadings of the Self. But it is fatally easy to delude ourselves. A marriage has become too difficult, for instance; we are not free, we say, to develop and grow as an individual because of the constant friction or the obtuseness of our partner, so loyalty to the Self demands separation. Maybe so, but first we must face the extremely difficult task of unraveling our unconscious motives (the silver key); and we must also be willing and humble enough to recognize as valid the objective wisdom of those whom we trust as interpreters of the inner voice of the Self (the golden key). This is most emphatically not a matter of blind obedience. The imaginative "following" already mentioned is relevant here. Whether we take or refuse the advice given by another, the vital point is that we hear it not only with our ears but with the deepest imaginative awareness of which we are capable. "So from her act, poured through the eyes into my imagination, my own action took shape."

Beatrice, moreover, gives us a hint of one way to test the validity of such a breaking of commitment. Be sure, she says, that the new way of life which you choose demands more of you than the old, in the proportion of six to four. How Dante's inexorable pinning down of vague aspiration to a defined reality shines out in these precise numbers! In other words, the breaking of a vow must be at its roots a sacrifice (a making holy), a movement towards wholeness, *not* an escape. Finally she points out the opposite danger—an obstinate clinging to the letter of a vow made foolishly and blindly.

As Jephthah pledged his first-met, and kept troth;

Whom more behoved to say: *I did amiss,*
Than keep it and do worse. . . .
       (V, 66–68)

Jephthah vowed to the Lord that he would sacrifice the first
thing he met after God should give him victory over his
enemies. He met his own daughter. One does not bribe the
Lord God with impunity. We do this whenever we consciously
or unconsciously assume we are owed something because of
our promises, whether made to God or man. How great then
is the need to be conscious all the time of the nature of every
commitment, large or small! Only then is a man truly free to
make or break them at will.

Mercury

D ANTE AND BEATRICE are transported with the swiftness of an arrow's flight to the next planet, Mercury.
Here Dante meets the souls of leaders among men
who, while truly devoted to God, nevertheless sought personal
glory. They are aptly placed on Mercury, as this planet is rarely
seen, being dimmed by its closeness to the sun—a figure of
the merging of personal light in the light of God.

Dante converses at length with the Emperor Justinian about
the history of Rome and the role of the Empire, which, for
Dante, was the symbol of the divine order in time; and Beatrice,
discerning in her love for him the questions in his mind which
he fears to ask, speaks to him about the paradox of history and
its relation to the justice of God, to Adam's fall, the Redemption, and the Atonement. Her words define for him, as far as
words may, the reality of both justice and grace, of man's full
and free responsibility and at the same time his total dependence. The Crucifixion, she says, was, in the deepest sense, an
"occasion for joy" (Charles Williams) in the Godhead; at the
time it was humanity's payment for the Fall, and on yet
another level it was a monstrous crime in those individuals
who committed it. So it is in all the phenomena of history—and
we may add, in every man's personal life. Hideous injustices
are everywhere and each crime breeds its own revenge, but
in that unimaginable totality which is God, in that core of man
which is both wholly human and wholly divine, all suffering
becomes innocent as was Christ's—no longer felt as a senseless misery or as a punishment for our guilts, but as a necessity
of the way of individuation, to which we consent. Thus our
God-given free will chooses the pain of which is born the
consciousness of the incarnate God within.

This is no impractical theory. Everyone may prove its truth
day by day even on what seems the most trivial level. Suppose
I feel rejected, humiliated, and perhaps indulge in anger against
another. "It is horribly unjust," I say; or else I fall into a
self-pitying sense of being no good, and so on. Then, if I am

of a psychological turn of mind, I will add, "Well, this is a compensation for my desire to be superior, special," etc. Quite right, of course. It is indeed the "just vengeance" of one opposite fighting the other, and this realization can be a step on the way, although often we are only trying to reason ourselves out of feeling bad. There is, however, another possible step into a detachment from both superior and inferior feelings, into a love and understanding of that weak, storm-tossed ego and shadow of mine and of the other, and so into acceptance of responsibility for them and of the pain that their struggles bring. We know the suffering then as a mercy, a grace, beyond the categories of just or unjust. If we can do this exceedingly difficult thing even for a moment, then for that moment we are suffering innocently and are, in however small a way, one with the atonement which is the Cross, and have known the meaning of the words, "His will is our peace."

Among those many whose fate has led them through the fire in great and terrible ways, a few rare people, to whom we owe deep gratitude, have written in our time of precisely this experience of suffering which becomes innocent and redemptive, being purged of all hatred, of all self-pity, of all ego-centered guilt. Julia de Beausobre is one, to whose book, *The Woman Who Could Not Die*, I have already referred in the chapter on Ante-Purgatory. Laurens Van der Post is another. In his book *The Seed and the Sower* he describes such cruelties of man to man as are almost unbearable to the imagination. Yet the book leaves one with no sense of bitterness or despair. On the contrary we are lifted out of all our small preoccupations and moved to a profound compassion for the torturer as well as for the victim, as we catch a glimpse of the absolute justice and mercy beyond the worst that unconscious humanity can do.

Before we leave Mercury I should like to return for a moment to the description of the arrival of the poet and Beatrice on this planet because it conveys so vividly that "feeling of the *Paradiso*" of which T.S. Eliot spoke. The following lines awaken us to awareness of four threads which are woven into the texture of the *Paradiso* from beginning to end. First we feel the excitement of the radiant joy which pervades the whole; then we note the human delight and interest of the redeemed in Dante as a person; thirdly we rejoice in Dante's own simple humanity in these high places, as his metaphors root us firmly and repeatedly on this earth; and lastly we realize once more how intensely he feels a personal relatedness to each one of his readers, as he confides in us with all the sincerity of his great and humble spirit.

> And O! such joy I saw my Lady wear
> When to that shining heav'n she entered in,
> The planet's self grew brighter yet with her;
>
> And if the star laughed and was changed, what then
> Was I, who am but flesh, and ticklish
> To touch of change, and all the moods of men?
>
> As in a fish-pond clear and still, the fish
> Draw to some dropped-in morsel as it moves,
> Hoping it may provide a dainty dish,
>
> So I saw spendours draw to us in droves,
> Full many a thousand, and from each was heard:
> "Lo, here is one that shall increase our loves!"
>
> And every shade approaching us appeared
> Glad through and through, so luminously shone
> Its flooding joy before it as it neared.
>
> Think, Reader, if this tale I have begun
> Broke off abruptly here, how thou wouldst fret,
> Wondering and wondering how it should go on,
>
> And judge by this how keen I was to get
> News of those beings there and then revealed,
> Of what they were, and in what station set.
>
> (V, 94–114)

The heart lifts and the reader may say to himself, "He is talking to *me*, not to *us*." It is as though Dante himself speaks personally to each passionate reader through the centuries, and says, as the "splendours" said to him, "Lo, here is one who shall increase our loves!" I recently read a description of a school mistress by one of her pupils. She succeeded, said the pupil "in putting such a salt and savour into life, that it seemed as if we could never think anything dull again" (J. Lash, *Eleanor and Franklin*, p. 81). These indeed are the marks of the great teacher in any age. They apply superlatively to Dante.

Venus

WITHOUT EVEN FEELING it, Dante is transported to Venus, seeing only the increased beauty in Beatrice's face. In Venus are the lovers; and the souls here appear to Dante as sparks, or gleams, wheeling in the heart of the light which is love, and singing "such Hosannahs that the ache to hear those songs again will haunt me till I die." Here we are immediately reminded of that other side of Venus in Hell, where we met Paolo and Francesca also whirling, but aimlessly, on the pitiless black wind; there, in place of the song of Heaven, "with cry and wail and shriek, they are caught by the gust."

"I am the center of a circle equidistant from every point on the circumference," said the personification of Love to the young Dante in a vision of which he wrote in the *Vita Nuova*. It was his first glimpse of the wholeness of love freed from dependence on anything the ego demands. Writing of the vision then, he found it obscure; but now in the light of Venus he comes back to the same image, and the circle remains with him as the supreme symbol of love. The whirling in Hell is without any center, simply the running round in circles of our neurotic desires, when we refuse the suffering of mature love; while the circling of the lovers in Heaven is the great dance of the spheres, to which this suffering may bring us.

> Then one alone approached us, crying clear:
> "We'd have thee glad of us, and to fulfil
> Thy whole desire we all stand ready here.
>
> Here, in one thirst, one wheeling, and one wheel
> We whirl with the celestial princes. . . ."
>
> (VIII, 31–35)

The one who speaks is Charles Martel, the young king of Hungary who died not long after his sojourn in Florence, where he became a true and beloved friend of Dante's. After

Fig. 36: Heaven of Venus

referring to the sad misrule of princes in Europe, including his own brother's mistakes, he explains in answer to Dante's questioning the vital importance of individuality, of differences in temperament, in capacity, in function, without which there can be no relationship between man and man, no society, and no community. The stars, he says, under God bestow on each man his natural gifts and propensities; if men on earth would bear in mind and strive to build on the foundation laid by nature,

"They'd have fine folk, with virtues all alive.

But you distort the pattern of the creature;
You cloister him that's born to wield the sword,
And crown him king who ought to be a preacher;

Thus from the path you wander all abroad."
　　　　　(VIII, 144–148)

The popularity of astrology today, superstitious though much of it may be, is proof that the stars are still powerful symbols for us, projection points for the unconscious, carrying a numinous power to evoke a sense of the natural "pattern" which is "given" to us at birth. Psychology from Freud onwards has given to modern man a tool for the rediscovery via the unconscious of this pattern, distorted and repressed as it so often is. Upon this "foundation laid by nature" a man must then build through the long effort of discriminating his own unique meaning and fate in life from the attitudes imposed on him by convention, by collective pressures, by his own desires and fears. Dante knew, as clearly as Jung did, that without this fidelity to nature *plus* conscious discrimination and discipline, there could be no individuation, and no real relationship between man and man.

This first meeting of Dante's on Venus was with a friend; his second is with a woman whom he had also probably known as a boy in Florence, when she was old and wise and revered for her compassion to all men. Her early life, however, had been colorful, to say the least. She had been the mistress of the troubadour poet Sordello, running away from her first husband. Tracked down by her brother, she again escaped with a knight and traveled, unmarried, about Italy with him. After his death she married again three times. Dante's description of her and her words is a lovely thing.

> And lo! another splendour now drew nigh,
> Eager to please, and showed me its intent
> Clearly, by growing brighter to the eye.
> . . . .
>   . . . this light, as yet unknown to me,
> Spoke, as it erst had sung, from its deep heart,
> As one delighted to give generously. . . .
>
>   (IX, 13–24)

She is, she tells him, Cunizza, sister of one of the most cruel tyrants in Italy.

> ". . . and I glitter here because
> I was o'ermastered by this planet's flame;
>
> Yet gaily I forgive myself the cause
> Of this my lot, for here (though minds of clay
> May think this strange) 'tis gain to me, not loss."
>
>   (IX, 32–36)

Here is Dante's most joyous and unequivocal assertion of the meaning of individual completeness. Cunizza is here in Venus and not higher in the hierarchy, because we enter into bliss with our entire personalities, not simply with our virtues. Our shadow qualities remain with us to the end; but when the responsibility for them is fully accepted, then they may be "gaily forgiven," and so be transformed and integrated until they are known as gain, not loss. To forgive ourselves "gaily" sounds easy, but it is in fact an extremely difficult thing, for it implies a rare kind of humility. When we achieve it, there will come the degree of bliss of which each one is capable but which is also, Dante pointed out at the beginning, ultimately one with all other levels of Paradise. Often we imagine we have forgiven ourselves when we have merely belittled or explained away the evil. Perhaps that very quality of true gaiety— lightness of heart—is the touchstone, for if we have not looked at and truly accepted the darkness, our so-called self-forgiveness may bring temporary relief, but always there is an increased sense of weight from the unconscious guilt, which sooner or later makes itself felt in repetition of the evil.

Cunizza had been overmastered by desire in the same way as Francesca in the first circle of the *Inferno*, and both of them have entered the eternal wheeling motion which is a symbol of desire on all levels. In other words, they experience the same things, but for one it is Heaven and for the other Hell. Nowhere in the poem is it more clearly seen that Heaven and Hell are not places but states of consciousness, with the clear implication that, as Jung so often said, the choice between them lies in the individual's conscious standpoint and willingness to confront his egocentricity. Francesca's desire remained centered on Paolo as a mere projection of her own inner longing; and she circles aimlessly, forever bound to his image. Cunizza, we may be sure, through long years of struggle and suffering had won through to the reality of relationship and compassion, and all her wandering desires had become one in the wheeling dance around the center which is Love itself.

The third soul who addresses Dante is that of a poet, the troubadour Foulquet, and he too speaks briefly of the torments of desire which he had experienced and which have been transmuted into the contemplation of this great Center. He also speaks of a fourth soul, "blazing amongst all these as sunbeams blaze from water sparkling clear." She is Rahab, the harlot of Jericho, who risked her life to save the spies of Joshua. Nothing could be plainer that this. She gave her body to many men but would have given her life for that of another in danger. Thus the harlot is in heaven; it is not the conventions but the quality of her love, the state of our innermost morality which determines our heaven or our hell.

It is surely not by chance that Dante meets four kinds of lovers in Venus—the true friend, the passionate unconventional woman, the poet, and the harlot, representing four types of total commitment. It does not ultimately matter whom we love. The only thing that matters is whether that love leads to increasing consciousness through sacrifice of the greed and safety of the ego, or whether it leads to a gradual swallowing up of the personality into the hell of concupiscence.

It is perhaps well to pause here in the planet of love and speak of an element in the *Commedia* with which we have been little concerned. The constantly repeated diatribes against the potentates of the Church and against the various secular rulers, most particularly those of Florence, are an essential element in the poem. All three of the souls here made perfect in love join in the chorus of condemnation, which is maintained in most of the spheres. For Dante, love is indeed far from an easy sentimental tolerance. Later, St. Peter in the topmost heaven delivers a shattering denunciation of Pope Boniface VIII and of the betrayal which he symbolizes, so that Heaven itself flushes red with anger and shame. The great difference between most violent exposures of evil and Dante's is that the former are made by people who have not been through Hell and Purgatory individually. Those who *have* made this journey and have emerged into acceptance and awareness of the totality do not on that account dissociate themselves from the battle of the opposites on other levels. They remain in the thick of it and openly express their feelings, mincing no words. Christ himself was no exception. Where they differ from the blindly unconscious rebels of the world is in their certainty of the Messiah: of the ultimate reconciling symbol which is already for them the reality by which they live. Those who think the *Paradiso* contains, beyond all change, no darkness, no concern with human conflict, are sadly mistaken.

The Sun

AFTER THE LOVERS in Venus, we arrive in the heaven of the thinkers. They stand in a circle of twelve lights around Dante and Beatrice, shining with overwhelming brilliance against the intense light of the sun—light upon light, Dante says, not color upon light. As canto X in the *Inferno* began the journey into nether Hell after the passage of the ramparts of Dis, and canto X in the *Purgatorio* followed the entry into Purgatory proper through Peter's Gate, so canto X in the *Paradiso* is the beginning of a new dimension of Heaven. We have passed beyond the tip of the conical shadow of earth, which was believed to reach as far as the sphere of Venus, and have come into the blazing light of consciousness which is the Sun. Here we meet twelve and later twelve more, making twenty-four, of those great men whose powerful intellects have been transformed by love into vehicles of wisdom through their total integrity and devotion to the truth as they perceived it.

Canto X opens with a great paean in praise of the Trinity and of that looking, gazing, contemplating, which is both knowledge and love:

> The uncreated Might which passeth speech,
> Gazing on His Begotten with the Love
> That breathes Itself eternally from each,
>
> All things that turn through mind and space made move
> In such great order that without some feel
> Of Him none e'er beheld the frame thereof.
>
> Look up with me, then, Reader, to the reel
> The exalted heavens tread, and scan that part
> Where one wheel crosses with the other wheel;
>
> There gaze enamoured on the Master's art,
> Whence never he removes the eye of Him,
> Such is the love He bears it in His heart.
>
> (X, 1–12)

Of the Trinity and Dante's intuition of the fourth we will speak later. Meanwhile there are no fewer than six verbs of "looking" in these brief verses. The Father gazes on the Son with the love which is the Holy Spirit proceeding from both. Man gazes on the superlative beauty of the order in the created universe, and inevitably he is "enamoured" by his vision of that upon which the Godhead also gazes with eternal love. When Dante asserts that God made all things in a perfect order, whether they circle within the mind or in physical space, it is surely a hint of that reality which both Jung in his theory of synchronicity and many modern physicists have approached in our time from a scientific standpoint.

A. Jaffe in her book, *From the Life and Work of C. G. Jung*, writes, "Synchronistic phenomena point to the existence of that acausal orderedness we have spoken of, to which both the observing psyche and the observed physical process are subject. The conception of an order anchored in the metaphysical realm places synchronicity, as a principle of cognition, within the framework of conformity to law that runs through the natural sciences; it is only a special instance, widely postulated today, of a transcendental order embracing the worlds within and without, spirit and cosmos. In Jung's own words, 'I incline in fact to the view that synchronicity in the narrower sense is only a special instance of general acausal orderedness—that, namely, of the equivalence of psychic and physical processes.'"[27] The two wheels that cross each other in Dante's imagery are the daily movement of the planets and the annual movement of the sun through the ecliptic. His *thought* could not, of course, go beyond the medieval framework of cause and effect; yet when we feel through the poetry the majesty of that contemplation, by God and man, of the circular reality of the universe, of "all things that turn through mind and space," moved by the "uncreated might," then we are very close to that equivalence of psychic and physical processes "anchored in the metaphysical realm" of which Jung wrote in the language of psychology and out of the vastly expanded state of intellectual consciousness today.

In this opening canto of the heaven of the Sun there is another fascinating instance of Dante's insight, pointed out by B. Reynolds in her notes. She says, "It is interesting to compare Dante's pleasure in the order of the universe with Milton's impassioned and rhetorical lines (*Paradise Lost*, X, 650 ff.) explaining how that same inclination (which Dante considers providential) [the ecliptic] was part of the Curse brought about by the Fall, whereas if Eve had left the apple alone, the temperate zone (in which Eden was situated) would have enjoyed 'Spring perpetual.'"[28] This attitude at once explains why Satan is sometimes felt to be the hero of *Paradise Lost* and God so very dull. For Dante the glory of order was joyously enhanced by its apparent flaws. (The ancient oriental rug makers would not make a carpet without a flaw.)

After this hymn to love and order, Dante plunges us into the light, the dazzling, unimaginable light of that which is brighter than the sun.

> And if imagination cannot run
> To heights like these, no wonder: no eye yet
> E'er braved a brilliance that outshone the sun.
>
> But such was God's fourth family, there set
> In endless joy, bathed by the Father's rays,
> Which show them how He breathes and doth beget.
> . . . .
>
> Ne'er was man's heart with such great eagerness
> Devoutly moved to make his whole self over
> To God, with all the will that in him is,
>
> Than at those words was I; I grew God's lover
> So wholly, needs must Beatrix' self admit
> Eclipse, and I became oblivious of her.
>
> But this displeased her not; she smiled at it,
> So that the splendour of her laughing eyes
> From one to many things recalled my wit.
>
>> (X, 46–63)

As so often, Dante, having drawn us with him into an almost unbearable ecstasy, restores us with lines like these last three to the solid earth of his human and personal relationship with Beatrice. She was laughing with him and at him. We remember suddenly that he is solid flesh and blood, one who knows the hells and purgatories of daily life and who casts a shadow of his own in this place, beyond the collective shadow of the world. So we may find courage to stand beside him in imagination and endure the blazing of the lights and the sound of their fiery song in our ears.

> . . . they who seek
> To hear them must find wings to reach that goal,
> Or wait for tidings till the dumb shall speak.

So carolling, that ardent aureole
Of suns swung round us thrice their burning train,
As neighbouring stars swing round the steady pole;
. . . .

Now from within one fire a voice arose. . . .
>   (X, 73–82)

The voice is that of St. Thomas Aquinas, whose teaching had been the wellspring of Dante's own thought.

We might expect here to be faced with long philosophical discourses, but although we are certainly obliged, as ever, by Dante to make the greatest effort of which we are capable to understand with our minds, yet the overwhelming impression left on us by these cantos is again of love—love which shines with a piercing light of truth. It becomes wholly clear as we read that, for Dante, learning which did not spring from love and lead to love in action was contemptible and worthless, belonging to the pit where Nimrod mouthed his meaningless jargon. For although the shining "intellectual," objective love of these cantos is in one sense beyond personal concerns, it is at the same time a great flowering of love between persons. Two whole cantos out of the four and a half devoted to this heaven are concerned with the personal lives and work of St. Francis and St. Dominic. The followers of these two saints were at loggerheads in Dante's time, and so they are honored here, in a great act of courtesy, the first by a Dominican, the second by a Franciscan.

St. Francis was concerned not at all with abstractions. He was a man of feeling who personified all his experiences, both inner and outer. To him Brother Wolf, Sister Water, Brother Pain, Sister Death, and "My Lady Poverty" were people to be known and loved personally. Human beings, birds, animals, trees and stones, thoughts and sensations, were all equally alive with meaning; and he lived in immediate personal relatedness with all of them. He did not think about meanings; he was directly aware of them. The Dominican, St. Thomas, who spent all his life defining, discriminating, and teaching the intellectual faith, pays homage to this man of the heart and the imagination; while the Franciscan, St. Bonaventure, in the harmony of courteous exchange, praises the integrity of mind, the princely intellectual courage of St. Dominic, the thinker and preacher in the service of truth.

In canto XIII, St. Thomas turns to philosophy and discourses on the nature of all creation as a reflection of God. He also makes an attempt to explain the problem of imperfection and evil. Like all such intellectual attempts it does not satisfy. It was, of course, impossible for Dante or any Christian thinker in that age to postulate a dark side of God. As a poet, however, as a man of intense intuitive and psychological wisdom, we feel him reaching down to this mystery.

In this same canto there is a fascinating instance of Dante's mistrust of too much intellect. The commentators have all been startled by the appearance of Solomon in a major role amongst all the doctors of the Church. St. Thomas had pointed him out earlier to Dante as

> . . . that mind majestical

> There dwells, in whom such wisdom did abound,
> None ever rose in any generation,
> If truth speak true, to insight so profound.

> (X, 111–114)

Now St. Thomas explains to Dante these words, saying that it was in *kingly* wisdom that Solomon had never been surpassed, which of course would mean the deep understanding of the human heart which a true king must have if he is to rule with justice and mercy. Solomon had asked God for a "wise and understanding heart," and so it seems that Dante with unerring vision gave a place of highest honor in this heaven of the intellect to a soul whose wisdom was of the heart and not the head.

St. Thomas' last message to Dante follows, and it is not a philosophical abstraction but a piece of sound psychological advice. "Do not make hasty judgments about either ideas or people," says St. Thomas, "by taking words out of context without the hard effort of discrimination."

> "For low among the dunces is his place
> Who hastens to accept or to reject
> With no distinction made 'twixt case and case;

> Thence come rash judgements, mostly incorrect
> And prejudiced, and stubborn all the more
> That self-conceit shackles the intellect."

> (XIII, 115–120)

When one has made a categorical assertion, vanity prevents one from backing down.

> "Worse than in vain does any quit the shore
> To fish for truth, the fisher's art unknowing—
> He'll not return the man he was before. . . ."
>
> (XIII, 121–123)

This has a very modern sound in our ears! If we go fishing in the unconscious without the art—the ability to discriminate—the unconscious will possess us and we shall emerge, if at all, changed indeed. Don't count your chickens before they are hatched, advises St. Thomas in an equally homely image:

> "No one should ever be too self-assured
> In judgement, like a farmer reckoning
> His gains before the corn-crop is matured,
>
> . . . .
>
> Let Jack and Jill not think they see so far
> That, seeing this man pious, that a thief,
> They see them such as in God's sight they are,
>
> For one may rise, the other come to grief."
>
> (XIII, 130–142)

Barbara Reynolds says, "From no one, as from Aquinas, had Dante learnt intellectual integrity." That the great thinker's last words to Dante should be concerned with the integrity of a man's judgment of his fellows as individuals in the sight of God is yet another moving example of Dante's sureness in the realms of thought and human relationship. As usual, after a soaring intellectual passage we are firmly dumped back into practical wisdom.

We come now to Dante's last conversation in the heaven of the intellectuals. It is not by chance that it is about the Resurrection of the Body, that great intuitive dogma of the Church; and it is most fitting that he is answered by Solomon, supposed author of the Song of Songs:

> "And when we put completeness on afresh,
> All the more gracious shall our person be,
> Reclothed in the holy and glorious flesh. . . ."
>
> (XIV, 43–45)

Thus speaks Solomon. Though projected outward and into a remote future, this is, like all the dogmas of the Church, the image of an ever-present and inward reality, remote because so deeply buried in the unconscious for most men. The spirit of man is not complete without the flesh. The infinite is not whole without the finite. There is ultimately one world, psychic and physical. Metaphysician, psychologist, and physicist move toward the same truth—that truth which has always been served by the wise among men. Here is the essence of true Christianity, so sadly betrayed in the distortions of the puritanical tradition. The "holy and glorious flesh" is not to be rejected but recognized as an essential part of eternal being.

In this century, as Jung pointed out so powerfully in *Answer to Job*, the dogma of the bodily Assumption of the Mother of God is a sign of the approach to consciousness of this ever-present though long repressed and misunderstood element. Mary is ultimately a symbol of all humanity, and the new-old dogma places her on a near equality to the Trinity, with her entire animal and human nature, as here, so in the "beyond." In the Trinity itself the feminine is already implicit; Christ was mystically known as androgynous, and the Holy Spirit is both the masculine sword of discrimination and the feminine wisdom of Sophia—the unity of these two being the love of both Father and Son. But the Assumption is the recognition of the feminine and material as a value distinct and eternal in itself, dwelling as *person* beyond time and space.

The emphasis of early Christianity on the masculine deity was essential if man's consciousness was to emerge from the pagan state of identity with the mother unconscious. In the Middle Ages, however, the stirring in the unconscious of the repressed feminine value, the dawning need for a new and far more conscious approach to the woman *within* as well as without are seen on all sides. In the Grail legends, for example, the inner quest is for the feminine vessel. The movement of courtly love, the cult of the Virgin, above all the searching of the alchemists and their vessel of transformation: all derive from the intuition of the lost value without which there can be no wholeness.

The opposites were to become still more widely split apart—the idealization of women and the cult of the pure Virgin leading to the phenomena of witches and witch hunts. In Dante there is no such split. The whole great drama of the poem begins from the human love of Dante for a girl who at the age of 18 was a miracle and a glory to him on a Florentine street. He never lived out his love with her in the flesh; and from the very first vision described in the *Vita Nuova*, he seems to have had an intuition of the great suffering through which he must pass, losing her in the flesh to find her as his inner guide, still herself—more herself than ever because she is his link to the Self.

It is to be remembered that Dante did not become an ascetic denying the flesh after his loss of Beatrice. He married and had children and loved other women; but Beatrice, the inner image, never became a spiritualized concept. As a woman she sends him down to the confrontation with evil in Hell and the long struggle towards consciousness in Purgatory; and as a woman still she now leads him through the deepest places of Paradise in his own body, toward that realization without which even the joyous spirits he meets in Paradise are not complete.

In the ultimate vision of the White Rose, Dante sees the blessed in their human bodily form. As he mounts higher from heaven to heaven they have appeared to him as lights, ever-increasing in the intensity of their radiance. We must remember the paradox that the souls in each heaven dwell also at the center, and that Dante is shown them in this way, step by step, because he *cannot* look on their wholeness without a long training in the ability to bear that ultimate light of consciousness. Before the ultimate unity is revealed to him, in a "point," in a single flash of awareness, Dante must gain strength to see the blessed not simply as lights but as "reclothed in the holy and glorious flesh."[29] How different from the world-denying spirituality which seeks release from the flesh and a dissolving of the personality in the light!

Fig. 37: Heaven of the Sun

Mars

HIGHER THAN THE heaven of those who gave the utmost devotion of their minds is the heaven of those who shed their blood with that same devotion. The poet finds himself in the ruddy glow of Mars, and he is so filled with joy and thankfulness that,

> With my whole heart, and in that tongue which all
> Men share, I made burnt-offering to the Lord,
> Such as to this new grace was suitable,
>
> And ere the sacrificial fire had soared
> Forth of my breast, I knew my prayer had sped
> Accepted. . . .
>
> > (XIV, 88–93)

Thus Dante links the wordless prayer of the *single* heart with the sacrifice of blood—for to pray inwardly in this total manner is precisely a death of the ego, a payment of "blood" symbolically, a sacrificial fire. It is a prayer that asks for nothing; and it brings, as always, on those rare occasions when we have the courage to desire it, a new insight, new vision.

Against the reddish light of the planet appears a great white cross:

> E'en so, constellate in the depth of Mars,
> Those rays displayed the venerable sign
> Traced in a circle by the quadrant-bars.
>
> Here memory beats me, and my wits resign
> Their office, for that cross so flashed forth Christ
> As beggars all similitude of mine. . . .
>
> > (XIV, 100–105)

It is not the usual Christian Cross of the Passion which gives him this sudden intuitive glimpse, but the equal-armed cross,

Fig. 38: Heaven of Mars

symbol of the quaternity. It seems that this experience of the
unity of love and thought, in the last heaven of the Sun, comes
to full expression in this mandala image "flashing forth Christ";
and a little later he speaks to the blessed of this unity:

> . . . "Love and intelligence
> Achieved their equipoise in each of you
> When first you saw the Prime Equivalence;

> Because that Sun which lit and warmed you through
> With heat and light, maintains preeminent
> A poise no likeness can do justice to."
>
> (XV, 73–78)

Against the pure white light of the cross Dante sees many
moving lights, like rubies, and from them comes a song of
which he heard almost nothing with his ears but which entranced him in the core of his being.

With their usual exquisite courtesy the souls cease their
singing so that Dante may speak, and one of the lights moves
swiftly like a shooting star to the foot of the cross. To Dante's
great astonishment, this soul greets him with the words, "O
blood of mine." It is Dante's own ancestor, his great-great-

grandfather, Cacciaguida, who is filled with great joy at seeing his descendant so blessed as to be brought here before his death.

This meeting is the heart of Dante's experience in the heaven of Mars, the red planet of blood. We do not find here, as might be expected, stories of the shedding of blood by martyrs and soldiers; but instead our attention is focused from the beginning on the *inner* significance of blood. First came the kind of prayer which is a blood sacrifice, and now we are led to meditate on the meaning of the blood tie to the ancestors.

There is a delightfully human moment here when Dante addresses his ancestor with the formal pronoun "you" of deep respect, which was very rarely used in his day.

> Beatrice smiled, standing a little off,
> As Guenevere's good dame, when the queen made
> Her first recorded slip, was moved to cough.
>
> (XVI, 13–15)

As Guenevere's lady-in-waiting tried to warn her of what she was up to with Lancelot by a cough, so Beatrice's smile warns him, but indulgently, of the temptation to pride in his descent. It would be interesting to study all the subtle nuances of Beatrice's smile along the way. Dante's repeated descriptions of the ever-increasing joy and beauty of her smile as she rises from heaven to heaven never become boring; it remains fresh and alive, a human smile on a human face to the topmost heavens.

After describing his own and Dante's origins and the good and simple life lived in Florence in the old days, Cacciaguida denounces the corruption of their city; and finally, in answer to Dante's questioning, he speaks in clear language of the poet's personal fate, predicting his exile, his loss of everything dear to him, his rejection by those he thought his friends, until he will be driven to stand quite alone, abandoning all parties. "Well shall it be for thee to have preferred making a party of thyself alone" (XVII, 68–69). Only then, he continues, will Dante find a true friend (Bartolommeo della Scala) whose courtesy is so deep and real that "It shall be Ask and Have between you, and the one most men put second, first shall be" (XVII, 74–75). In other words, with a true friend we have before we ask. "When one man stands alone he finds a companion," says the *I Ching*.

Dante affirms strongly that this foreknowledge which Cacciaguida sees pictured in the mind of God is in no way a denial of man's free will. In six brief lines he asserts the paradox of free will and fate:

"Contingence, which doth exercise no right
Beyond that frame of matter where you lie,
Stands all depicted in the Eternal Sight,

Though suffering thence no more necessity
Than doth the vessel down the river gliding
From its reflection in the watcher's eye. . . ."

(XVII, 37–42)

We could say that that which a man will choose on this level of cause and effect already exists in eternity, but that at the moment of choosing in time we are entirely free either to accept consciously our destiny, in which case every outer event means a step towards wholeness, or else to be swallowed by this same destiny into a state of disintegration and possession by unconscious forces. Outwardly Cacciaguida predicts the events of Dante's life; inwardly at the same time we feel the inevitable stripping down of a man who has accepted the "quest," until he dares to let go of all "parties," of all demands, of all collective support of any kind, so that naked and alone he accepts responsibility, not only for his actions and choices, but for his *fate*. Then indeed he will find the inner Friend, the symbol of the Self, and all will be given to him without the need of asking ("that which most men put second, first shall be").

We have now arrived at canto XVII, the half-way point of the *Paradiso*, and it is especially significant that here we meet with Dante's ancestor and the affirmation of his roots, his inheritance by blood. In all primitive societies, as also in myths and fairy stories, this theme of the heir is of basic significance. In the Grail legend, for example, Perceval discovers his blood relationship to the Grail King and to the Grail bearer when he is finally able to ask the vital question about the meaning of the Grail; and it is implied from the beginning that he was born with this fate because he was of the blood of the King. This is one of the greatest of innumerable stories of the unknown or dispossessed heir. A king is born of the blood royal and without it he is no king. In *The Lord of the Rings* by Tolkien, enormous emphasis is laid on the pure blood of the inherited kingship of Aragorn. It is of equal importance with the long training and purging of his personality for his vocation as king.

Cacciaguida attributes the degeneration of Florence to the pollution of her *blood* by a "low brood" of people from outside (an image of psychic invasion in our terms) and Dante's own constantly asserted belief that all allegiance to a true Emperor would cure the disorders in the secular world surely sprang from a projection of the inner truth that the authority of the "king," the representative of the Self in the psyche, is inherited in the "life blood," not made.

In the Christian creed the son of the Father is "begotten not made," and the Son was the King of Kings. Thus the dogma again formulates a fundamental pattern of the psyche. Emma Jung and Marie Louise von Franz, in their book on the Grail Legend, said that the King carried the archetype of wholeness in the ideal form in which it was possible to that age to glimpse it. As consciousness increases, one "king" (one attitude to the Self) dies and another will succeed. The "King of Kings," being the origin and end of all things, is fundamentally the only valid ruler in the psyche—the ruler from whom all men unconsciously seek to trace their descent. Hence the immense importance of the ancestors in primitive thinking, because they represent the unbreakable inheritance through generation after generation of the blood, the life essence, of the original "great man" of the tribe; or, as we should say, the great man in the psyche who is the Self, "begotten," not made by the ego. It is something given, not earned. Even today where kingship survives symbolically, as in Britain, it would be unthinkable for anyone to carry that symbol who was not of the blood royal. A true king is born, never made by the wishes of men; so also is the Royal Self in each of us.

It is easy to see the extreme danger of modern man's refusal to make conscious the profound inner meaning of this archetype of the "pure blood." This blindness is at the root of all race hatred and such horrors as the pure Aryan doctrines of the Nazis. We can no longer naively believe in the virtues of rulership based on inherited physical blood, but worship of equality *on the wrong level* and repression of the image of the king has done nothing to free mankind from persecutions on a most horrible scale; and we have seen how the unconscious will throw up an all-powerful dictator whose ego has swallowed the king archetype whole. In a kind of mass hypnosis people identify with both the blood royal and the slave.

Dante's hope that an Emperor true to his blood might arise who would restore harmony and world order seems naive to us; but he never made our fatal mistake of substituting collective ideals for the individual quest, nor did he confuse the personal ego of a Pope or an Emperor with his symbolic role. Dante's hopes for world order were ultimately rooted in the great story he told of the individual soul's journey to consciousness.

So, as we have learned to expect from him, Dante, here at the midpoint of the *Paradiso*, turns back from his discussions of the great matters of history and of mankind to the immediate and the personal. He establishes his own blood-tie of both flesh and spirit to this ancestor in a state of bliss—the Great Man, we could say, in his own psyche—and through this meeting he learns to accept the hard facts of his unique destiny in this world and his vocation as poet. Cacciaguida's last words to him are a final sweeping away of all caution and fear about telling just exactly what he has seen on this his journey into reality, no matter what the consequences to himself.

Make thy whole vision freely manifested,
And where men feel the itch, there let them scratch!
    (XVII, 128–129)

Jupiter

D ANTE AND BEATRICE now rise from the red planet to the clear white serenity of Jupiter, the place of justice where they meet the souls of the just lawgivers of mankind. Peace and order on earth is the theme which now absorbs the poet. Here the brilliant lights of the spirits form themselves into the shapes of letters and spell out the words *"Diligite justitiam qui iudicatis terram"* ("Love justice, ye who judge the earth"). Many other lights now come to join those that formed the last letter "m" of "*terram*," and gradually as in a dance they transform it into the image of a brilliantly shining eagle, the symbol of justice and the order of Roman law.

It is interesting that Jupiter is the only sphere in which Dante does not converse with an individual; the voice of the Eagle itself speaks to him. In some exquisite lines he conveys to us the awareness of many distinct individuals speaking with a single voice. When the one authority in each soul is the will of God (the rule of the Self, in our words), then there is an end to disagreements about what constitutes justice, and the many speak the single sound. The "we" becomes "I," and yet each single "I" remains distinctly itself.

> Grandly before me, with its wings displayed,
> The image shone, which, in their sweet fruition
> Exultant, all those weaving spirits made;
>
> . . . .
>
> What I must now relate was ne'er with ink
> Written, nor told in speech, nor by the powers
> Of mind e'er grasped, to imagine it or think;
>
> For I beheld and heard the beak discourse,
> And utter with its voice both *Mine* and *Me*,
> When in conception still 'twas *Us* and *Ours*.
>
> . . . .

As many coals are felt to shed all round
One glow of heat, so from that image went,
Blended of many loves, a single sound.

      (XIX, 1–21)

These lines make clear that Dante is not describing the ordinary
agreement of many souls speaking in unison, or a lot of people
submerging their individuality under a leader. For that image
would be a parrot, not an eagle. He is again trying to convey
a mystery—the great mystery of the simultaneous reality of the
many and the one. A little further on he exclaims,

Like to the lark which soars into the sky
Singing at first, and then, with utter bliss
Filled to the full, falls silent by and by,

So seemed to me yon image of the impress
Of that eternal Will by Love whereto
Each thing becomes that which it really is. . . .

      (XX, 73–78)

Dante is to learn in this heaven the unfathomable nature of the
justice of God. To our reason it seems that this man is worthy

Fig. 39: Heaven of Jupiter

of salvation and that other not; this historical event seems evil, another good, and indeed the one voice of the Eagle denounces the faithless rulers of mankind. But in the final vision of God we shall know the divine justice for the all-embracing thing it is; for it is something the human mind cannot comprehend, though it may know with certainty that it exists.

> Such vision, then, as you on earth receive
> Drowns in eternal Justice evermore,
> Like sight in ocean, whelmed beyond retrieve;
>
> For while it sees the bottom near the shore;
> In the great main no bottom's to be seen,
> Though it is there; the deep has sealed it o'er.
> (XIX, 58–63)

The six lights of the eye of the eagle are all great kings—David, Trajan, Hezekiah, Constantine, William II of Sicily, and Rhipeus the Trojan. Dante is amazed at the inclusion of two pagans, Trajan and Rhipeus—so much so that he causes the Eagle of souls considerable amusement.

> Amazement showed through me as clear as clear,
> To hold my peace was more than I could do;
>
> So that a cry burst forth, "What's this I hear?"
> As though its own weight forced my lips asunder.
> This roused great sparkling and much joyous cheer. . . .
> (XX, 80–84)

The Eagle answers, and it is plain that Dante has grown to the point where he can break out of the rigid externalized doctrines of medieval Christianity and penetrate to their inner meaning. Speaking of Rhipeus the voice says,

> "The other, by a grace from such deep ground
> Gushing that no created eye can plumb
> Its hidden well-springs where they run profound,
>
> On righteousness spent all his earthly sum
> Of love; whence God from grace to grace unsealed
> His eyes to the redemption yet to come.
> . . . .

Ere ever baptism was, a thousand year,
He was baptised. . . ."

(XX, 118–128)

This is a hint of the truth proclaimed by Julian of Norwich in
the words, "When Adam fell, God fell into his mother's womb."
Dante has seen that any man in any age may come to the vision
of the truth, though he has never heard of the historical
Christ—and in that moment he is "baptized," immersed in the
holy water of the unconscious from which is born the consciousness of the whole. Barbara Reynolds comments, "It would
appear from this that Dante's faith had broadened and deep-
ened during his later years and that he came to know, and to
rejoice in the knowledge, that Christian truth was not bounded
by his understanding."[30]

Saturn

THIS IS THE last and highest of the seven planets on Dante's journey, and in it are the souls of the contemplatives, of those who withdrew from the world to a life of prayer and contemplation.

> Coloured like gold which flashes back the light,
> I saw a ladder raised aloft so far
> It soared beyond the compass of my sight.
>
> Thereupon I saw descend from bar to bar
> Splendours so numerous I thought the sky
> Had poured from heaven the light of every star.
>
> (XXI, 28–33)

The golden ladder was a traditional symbol of contemplation deriving from Jacob's vision of the ladder between earth and heaven. Those who reached the contemplative vision of God were seen as ascending to that vision and descending again among men through their compassion. So also, in the East a Buddha is an enlightened one who chooses to stay in this world out of compassion. Dante here emphasized the soul's *descent*, as though they came down especially from the Empyrean to reveal themselves to him at his level of consciousness. Vividly he compares the "splendours," the flashing lights, to jackdaws in the dawn flying out and wheeling back to their perches, warming their feathers in the rising sun.

Here, amongst those whose vision is so deep, Beatrice does not smile.

> . . . "Were I to smile",
> Her words began, "thou would'st become the same
> As Semelè, burned to an ashy pile."
>
> (XXI, 4–6)

che la prima cagion non veggion tota

Fig. 40: *Heaven of Saturn*

Semelè (mother of Dionysus) was rash enough to ask Zeus to show himself to her in his true divinity and was immediately burned to ashes. Such indeed is the danger to anyone who, while still in an immature state, tries to penetrate to the archetypal powers hidden in the unconscious; a weak ego can be driven to insanity. Dante, as we have seen, insists continually on this tempering of the light to his capacity for vision, and on the peril of seeing too much too fast. Beatrice does not smile again until after Dante's glimpse of Christ in the next heaven when she says:

> "Lift up thine eyes and look on me awhile;
> See what I am; thou hast beheld such things
> As make thee mighty to endure my smile."
>
> (XXIII, 46–48)

In the traditional teaching of the Church, as in all the great religions, the contemplative life has always been valued above the life of action or life of the intellect. In the East, of course, there has never been any question about it, but since the

Reformation in the West the emphasis on the active life has grown and grown until even the Catholic Church is fast moving away from its original attitude. Everywhere we see the ancient priorities reversed. Martha, it is implied, even if this is denied in words, must now take precedence of Mary. Most people are driven to exhaustion by the ever-increasing demands made upon them for action in all its aspects, so that their first obligation, their overwhelmingly most important responsibility, to set up the ladder between man and God, between earth and the beyond, between conscious and unconscious, takes the last place. Even those who are aware of this responsibility, especially priests, are defeated by the sheer pressure of collective opinion and demand which leaves them too exhausted for the inner quietness of their vocation.

This trend is undoubtedly due to the fact that in this age we must either confront the opposites individually or die. No longer can the active and contemplative ways in the psyche be lived in compartments; nor can the inner life of the golden ladder be carried by projection onto monks, nuns, or holy men withdrawn from life, who in the past were symbols of these things for others. The answer is not a matter of swinging back again from overemphasis on activity to a cult of mysticism or a retreat from the realities of the outer world, as many have supposed. The individual has to find his solitary way to the equipoise, but there are great and wise guides, and not only in this century. Dante assuredly is such a one.

Gerhard Adler has written of this problem: "Patient and analyst are always confronted with this twofold question: the question of the meaning of our subjective inner personal life and the question of the meaning of the collective social life. These two aspects of meaning are intimately interconnected. On the one hand, the collective-social problems are bound to exert their influence on us and, on the other hand, we are always challenged to make our contribution, however small, to the collective-social situation around us."[31] We cannot separate ourselves from the state of the world, but that state depends ultimately on the awareness of individuals. Each man must discover for himself the degree of involvement in outer activity demanded of him at the different stages of his life. Adler concludes his essay, "Thus analysis (in Jung's sense), a tiny, apparently helpless factor when measured by world events, may yet contribute to building the bridge that will lead us across the abyss to a new and regenerated humanity, one which finds its meaning in a true humanism, in a genuine relatedness of man to man which is rooted in man's relatedness to his own psyche, itself rooted in unfathomable depths."[32]

In the *Paradiso* especially (though also from the very beginning, as has been pointed out), Dante is the poet of contemplation, not as opposed to action, the value of which he constantly reasserts, but in the sense of seeing, understanding, contemplating with insight, that which is behind all action and gives it its only meaning. If we are not able to contemplate our activity objectively, *sub specie aeternitatis*, a thing which can only be done if we are striving for individuation (by whatever name we call it), then it is all meaningless.

Over and over again he repeats it: "Look, look well." We spoke of this in the *Purgatorio*, but in the *Paradiso* one feels almost drunk with the richness of the verbs of looking. We noticed them in the chapter on the heaven of the Sun, and there are four such words in the two lines quoted above, "Lift up thine eyes and look. . . ." The examples are endless. Krishnamurti, in his book *Freedom from the Known*, has beautifully expressed the nature of this looking which is contemplation. Looking and listening are one thing, he says. We can come to its fullness only when we are completely free of the *demand* to be happy, to be anything other than what we are in this moment. The instant we demand a good thing, its evil opposite is immediately present. When, for instance, we feel jealousy or anxiety, we must neither accept it nor reject it but "care for it as you would care for a newly planted tree. . . . care for it, not condemn nor justify it. When you care for it you are beginning to love it. It is not that you love being envious or anxious, as so many people do, but rather that you care for watching."[33] To us in the West this is not enough because it is impossible for us to care for and love an abstract state without immediately getting caught in the head. Jung has given us the answer to this: if we will personify the emotion, then we can truly care for, look at, and so love, that jealous or anxious person within us. The unconscious speaks in images, not in concepts. Krishnamurti continues, ". . . when you look totally you will give your whole attention, your whole being, everything of yourself, your eyes, your ears, your nerves. You will attend with complete self abandonment. . . ."[34] This total attention to every smallest thing is the contemplative life.

Here in the heaven of Saturn a soul speaks to Dante of the essence of contemplation:

"Bearing directly on me is God's light,
Piercing the bowel of my being through.

Its power being then conjoined to my sight
Lifts me above myself until I gaze
Upon His essence whence is milked such might.

Thence comes the joyfulness wherewith I blaze;
My sight's intensity these sparklings show,
Thus flame with vision in the balance weighs."

(XXI, 83–90)

It is "His essence" which we see in every smallest fact, the moment we sacrifice demand and so are able to attend. One begins to understand something of what Simone Weil meant when she wrote about "looking and eating." I cannot quote the passage exactly, but she says in effect that when looking and eating become one thing, we shall be whole. I imagine that her meaning is that when we are *nourished* by looking (in the contemplative sense) and do not have to devour, possess, and so identify our egos with our experience, then the "light of God" is "conjoined" to our human sight, and we see and are one.

Contemplation, then, is not a separation from action, as every true contemplative and mystic has known; it is rather an attitude to both action and stillness, by which at the last they are one. "At the still point, there the dance is" (T. S. Eliot, *The Four Quartets*). If a man is to come to his individual identity he must, then, constantly put first the necessity to look at, to contemplate, everything that comes to him from within or from without in its relation to the Whole, as far as is possible to him day by day. This is the meaning of detachment as opposed to withdrawal. The majority put this necessity last and say, "There is no time." The ancient priority stands. Mary it was who chose the essential.

The Fixed Stars

GEMINI

AFTER A BRIEF conversation with St. Benedict, founder of Western contemplative monasticism, Dante rises with Beatrice to the sphere of the fixed stars and finds himself, appropriately, in the constellation of Gemini, his birth sign of the zodiac. In other words, he has come to the root of his own individual nature under God. He speaks to the stars themselves:

> O stars of glory, from whose light on high
> A mighty virtue poureth forth, to you
> I owe such genius as doth in me lie;
> . . . .
>
> To you my soul devoutly breathes, her source
> Of strength and power for the hardest phase
> Of all her journey towards which now she draws.
>
> (XXII, 112–123)

The literal translation is "My soul now breathes with devotion to you that she may win strength for the hard way which draws her to itself," and the Italian is a joy.

> A voi divotamente ora sospira
> l'anima mia, per acquistar virtute
> al passo forte che a sé la tira.
>
> (XXII, 121–123)

Dante is not writing superstitiously about the stars. He sees the origins of his God-given uniqueness in this symbol with awe and thankfulness. The image-destroying rationality of the modern world has inevitably produced such things as the superstitions of popular astrology, because we long—how we

et pero disubstanza prende intenza

Fig. 41: Heaven of the Fixed Stars

long!—for the experience of those inner stars of glory, our source of strength and power. It would be hard to address such lovely words to the genes, which is our modern word for the sources of our personality. Yet in fact they are as wonderful and mysterious as the stars. The divorce of science from the poetic spirit is the deadly thing. As was said earlier, some scientists, like Loren Eisely and Teilhard de Chardin, have bridged the gap.

Dante turns again to look at Beatrice. She stands, he says, like a bird in the early dawn which has sat patiently on her nest with her fledglings through the dark night, and now, perched on a high twig, eagerly awaits the sun so that she may bring them food. So Beatrice, poised, eagerly watches the horizon, knowing that a pageant of Christ and his triumphal hosts will appear for her friend Dante, who is also, as it were, her fledgling longing for this rich food.

Many have commented, often derogatively, on the mother-child aspect of the relationship between Beatrice and Dante. There is, in fact, no true feminine feeling which does not include the nourishing maternal element, which is quite another thing from a possessive and destructive mothering. The anima, the inner woman who opens the unconscious to men, carries the image of mother as well as friend, beloved, and goddess.

In the earthly Paradise Dante had seen in a pageant the Gryphon, an allegorical figure of Christ in his two natures such as could speak to his state of consciousness at that time. Now, having reached this highest point of the visible universe, he sees another pageant. Beatrice speaks:

> . . . "Behold Christ's hosts in triumph! Thou
> Mayst see the fruit all garnered here above
> Which 'neath these circling stars matured ere now."
>
> (XXIII, 19–21)

In this pageant Dante no longer needs the mediation of actors portraying allegorically in collective images the nature of Christ and of reality. Here he knows in a single moment of vision the one reality of all souls whom he had seen below step by step, and as we too, when we come to maturity, shall also see as one all the garnered fruit of our experience in time. Then Dante, in a flash as of lightning, glimpses the true substance of the living Christ. The vision is quickly withdrawn, for he cannot yet see and know it as he will in the last canto.

> Outshining myriad lamps, One Sun I knew
> Which kindled all the rest, even as our sun
> Lights the celestial pageantry we view.
>
> And through the living radiance there shone
> The shining Substance, bright, and to such end
> Full in my face, my vision was undone.
>
> O Beatrice! beloved guide, sweet friend!
>
> (XXIII, 28–34)

He cries out to her as to a lifetime in so great an ecstasy, and tries then to describe it:

> As fire from a cloud must soon explode,
> If it dilate and prove untenable,
> And downward flies, against its natural mode,
>
> My soul, grown heady with high festival,
> Gushed and o'erbrimmed itself; and what strange style
> It then assumed, remembers not at all.

. . . .

> I was as one that out of dreaming brings
> Nothing to mind, though fruitlessly he cast
> About, in search of hints and vanishings. . . .

(XXIII, 40–51)

Now Dante speaks once more of the overwhelming nature of that theme he must try to convey and reminds us of his warning at the beginning of the *Paradiso*.

> No sea for cockle-boats is this great main
> Through which my prow carves out adventurous ways,
> Nor may the steersman stint of toil and pain.

(XXIII, 67–69)

Recalled by Beatrice, he looks again and now sees the Virgin Mary—"that living star, who, as on Earth, in Heaven rules anew." The star was sapphire-blue in color, and Heaven itself was "made more gay" by its radiance. Mary now follows her son into Heaven, and all the other radiances follow like children clinging in love to their mother.

The vision over, Beatrice pleads with the souls in the eighth heaven, as they dance "whirling about fixed centers, circle-wise," to feed Dante crumbs from their table of joy. There follows the one great specific gateway of the *Paradiso*—a transition point of the kind we met with in the other two realms. Dante is almost ready to pass beyond the constellations and the entire visible universe to the sphere of the angels, the Primum Mobile, whence time originates, and from there to the Empyrean, where time and space are transcended. But first he must pass an entrance examination. He has moved in wonder and awe through all the levels of consciousness; he has looked and listened and labored to understand; but before he is lifted into the final realization, he must be able to *express* his deepest insights. He must define his understanding of the three essential virtues or states of being: Faith, Hope, and Love. The examiners are St. Peter, St. James, and St. John.

Here is a great truth which is valid at every stage of the quest. If we refuse or are not able to express, to make actual in some form or other our vision, such as it is at any point, then we are not only unable to go forward to the next step but are probably in for a regression. For instance, a dream or vision will retreat again into the unconscious and have no substance unless written or perhaps painted—made visible, audible, or tangible in some way—shared with one other, and attended to so that it alters our attitude. For a young man at the beginning of the way, this necessity of making incarnate his vision is as vital as it was for Dante in the eighth heaven. Perceval, for instance, seeing the great wonders of the Grail castle for the first time, found that it was not enough to *feel* a great yearning to know the meaning. He failed to alter anything because he did not make this yearning audible; he did not dare to break through the conventional code he had been taught and actually ask the vital question. His vision disappeared, and it would be many years before he could find it again. Moreover, as the maiden he met afterwards told him, many disasters would flow from his failure. The fact that he was too young and immature to ask the question made no kind of difference to the consequences. It is here seen that the making real of our visions can hang on something as simple as the asking of the right question out loud—that is to say, in a manner which affects our actual lives.

For Dante the test lay in whether or not he could express the essence of his long journey. He was a poet by vocation and to write these things in poetry was his agony of creation, his making incarnate of his vision. It must be remembered, of course, that it is not a matter of an intellectual exercise but of a creative act involving the whole man. He stood on the threshold of direct awareness of the ultimate unity, and no amount of knowledge or feeling or ecstatic experience of faith and hope and love was enough to take him across this threshold unless he could pass the test. So it is for every man, however simple and undramatic the vehicle of expression may be for most of us. The word must be made flesh by creation in this world.

The brilliant light which is St. Peter approaches, and it is Beatrice who asks him to examine Dante. "What is faith?" he says; and Dante begins by quoting St. Paul:

"The substance of things hoped for faith must be,
And argument of things invisible,
And this I take to be its quiddity."
     (XXIV, 64–66)

In the King James Version, the translation is the "evidence of things not seen," whereas in the Vulgate the word used is "argument." Dante goes on to explain that when we are faced with the mysteries of Heaven which are invisible to mortal eyes, we can experience them only through faith, which is the "substance" of hope—*sub-stance*, that which stands under it, so to speak, and is the essence from which all true hope springs. Moreover every "argument" (that is, talk *about* the mystery) is verified by faith alone.

We must now distinguish clearly between the so-called theological virtues and the ordinary view of these qualities as simply one side of a pair of opposites. There is a kind of so-called faith which is the opposite of doubt and easily degenerates into a lot of half-baked beliefs which are merely a protection against the agony of doubt and against the loneliness of individual thought and feeling. Doubt, on the other hand, may in its turn become an evasion of the frightening responsibility of real faith. But the way to the kind of faith without which we cannot ever know reality lies straight through the middle of doubt.

> . . . and doubt is still the lure
> That speeds us toward the height from crest to crest.
>   (IV, 131–132)

The inner virtue of Faith has nothing whatever to do with unreasoning acceptance of authoritarian sets of rules and beliefs, nor with its opposite delusion of emotional possession by spiritual experiences. We could define it, on the contrary, as the essential quality of a truly open mind. It is the kind of attitude of which Jung gave us such a superlative example. He was indeed above all things a man of true Faith; which is to say that he accepted as real every experience of the psyche, however irrational, however mysterious, without identifying with it. This faith in the totality of life, no matter how limited our knowledge, is the underpinning, the substance, of his entire work, through which indeed breathes a mighty wind of hope, and on which is based all his "argument," his reasoning about the unconscious. When someone asked Jung, towards the end of his life, "Do you believe in God?" he answered, "I do not believe, I know." He was not referring, of course, to intellectual knowledge; he was affirming that Faith which is the certain "evidence of things not seen." If we do not have this kind of faith we might as well forget about individuation, for we shall be incapable of freeing ourselves from collective attitudes.

We are apt to be confused by the paucity of language here. As the word "love" has so many meanings on different levels, so has the word "faith." Jung often wrote in condemnation of "faith," using the word in the sense of a blind belief which destroys intellectual honesty. This alters not at all the fact of his burning Faith as described above. John Sanford defines it as follows: "Faith is the state of consciousness which results from coming into relationship with a numinous divine reality. If your consciousness has been seized by God you have *faith*, then you really *know* deep in your heart and act accordingly, even though this knowledge has not been the result of an intellectual process."[35] I would lay stress here on the two words "relationship" and "consciousness," for it is very easy to mistake a mere state of possession by unconscious contents for faith. Relationship is a conscious state. This is the faith which Jung affirmed when he said, "I do not believe, I know that God exists."

Faith is the quality which gives birth to the creative imagination, and without it we are possessed by sterile materialism plus unconscious superstition and are dominated by puerile opinions. Without imaginative faith in that which is still unconscious, consciousness cannot expand. For instance, Jung, writing about the technique of active imagination, says in effect that it will be of no help to us if we do not wholly accept the validity of our most childish-seeming imagery. Faith is, in fact, imagination accepted as substance, breathing life into all our "argument." It then becomes sure "evidence" of the inexpressible mystery of life.

So also Dante, within the framework of medieval thought, affirms the same underlying truth. Faith, he says, is the root from which the definitions and arguments of theology spring. To subscribe blindly to things written and taught never creates faith; whereas once we have come to that very hardly attained openness of mind and heart, we are able to recognize the paradoxes of inner truth, and all our definitions reach down into that other dimension where the symbol gives them life.

"The mysteries of Heaven", I replied,
"Here manifested, as my sight perceives,
Are to our mortal eyes on earth denied;

Hence their existence faith alone conceives,
And hope's foundation thus doth represent,
Wherefore the name of *substance* it receives.

And from this faith, of things not evident
Our reasoning may proceed; therefore I see
Why it is designated *argument*."
                (XXIV, 70–78)

The order of St. Peter's questions is significant. First he asks, "What is faith?" and secondly, "Have you understood the meaning of St. Paul's words?" Dante's answer is quoted above. The third question is "Do you have it in your purse?" The form of this question may give us pause. We carry money in our purses, and money is the symbol of the values by which we live. Our actual use of money is clear evidence of the priorities in our lives; and when we dream of money we are given clues as to the unconscious use we are making of our psychic energy, of the nature of our exchanges. No one comes to true self-knowledge without a searching honesty about his attitude to money. Here St. Peter is saying in effect, "Is Faith the *coinage* of your life—the value that you bring to all your giving and taking? Are you free of that possessiveness which kills the beauty and freedom of exchange between man and man?

The qualities which distinguish a man of imaginative faith are trustfulness and trustworthiness. If a person is constantly suspicious of other people's good faith, it is quite certain that he is dominated by some brand of collective opinion and has a closed mind, however much he inveighs against "the collective." Equally, if a man has a blind belief in everyone's goodness and is continually taken in, he has not begun to discover the clear-eyed trust which is born of faith. For only through faith do we perceive the individual and come to the inner certainties which inspire trust in and from others.

"Do you have it in your purse?" Dante's poetry even is not enough (indeed it would not be true poetry) if he is merely speaking about faith. Is it a certainty of his soul by which he lives?

I answered: "Yes; and 'tis so round and bright
No doubt as to its mintage do I nurse."
                (XXIV, 86–87)

He knows that he has this coin because of its *roundness*; therefore he does not believe, he knows. Faith has no beginning or end; it does not come and go; it is therefore symbolized by the round coin or precious stone, as St. Peter calls it when he asks his fourth question, "Whence came this jewel to you?"

Dante answers that the Holy Spirit breathing through the Scriptures was the argument which cut the jewel, giving it both form and content—making it, that is, visible and tangible to his consciousness. This emphasis on the Scriptures, on the age-old wisdom written down by the wise and holy of the past, is not peculiar to Christianity and Judaism. It is an essential teaching in all the great religions of the East as well as of the West. It is no less valid for the individual seeker today. It emphatically does not imply a blind acceptance, but we do not exist in an isolated moment of time; without our roots in the ancestors of the spirit we are apt to be swept away by every "wind of doctrine." Their wisdom must be reinterpreted in our own language, not ignored.

St. Peter probes further. "How did you recognize the Spirit of Truth in the Scriptures?" he asks, and Dante replies that they speak of things which are beyond the cause and effect laws of nature. St. Peter, however, is not satisfied. "You can't prove the truth of a thing on the evidence of that thing itself." Dante tries again. He points to the evidence of the great miracle of change wrought in the lives of great numbers of people. In effect he repeats Tertullian's *"Credo quia impossible est."* Mere beliefs are powerless to alter radically the lives of men; only the transforming power of the basic truths of the psyche can do that. This is Dante's evidence. The truth is not just something theoretical; it is something that *works*.

St. Peter now asks his last question. Dante must express the ultimate content and origin of his faith. He replies:

"One God, eternal, sole, my creed doth know,
Mover of Heavens, being Himself unmoved. . . ."
     (XXIV, 130–131)

And he goes on to say that physics, metaphysics, and the outpouring of the Spirit in prophets and seers all speak the proofs, but the source is in the mystery of the Three Persons in the Godhead, who is also One, beyond all argument.

"This the beginning is and this the spark
Which, like a living flame, doth now dilate,
Shining within me like a star at dark."

(XXIV, 145–147)

The examination on Hope is much shorter, largely because Beatrice delightfully intervenes as soon as St. James poses his questions. "What is Hope? Does Dante have it? Whence did it come to him?" She answers the second question for him, saying that he possesses this quality in the highest degree and that the proof of it is his presence in this place of light. She is saving his modesty by speaking for him; and the other two questions, she knows, will give him little trouble. Dante replies with a great paradox. "'Hope', I began, 'is certainly of bliss to come, which God by grace to us concedes. . . .'" That hope which is a "certainty" is born on the other side of the petty optimism which is the opposite of fear and despair. Just as the virtue of Faith arises from the tensions between belief and doubt, so the virtue of Hope will come to us out of that Faith when we have known the illusions of transitory hope and the emptiness of despair and passed beyond. From the open mind of Faith springs that indestructible certainty of Hope whereby we are able to imagine wholeness, however dimly. As he ended his reasoning about Faith with the image of a flame shining like a star at dark, so he brings alive his answers to St. James in another living metaphor:

". . . in thine own epistle thou didst so
Instill me with his dew that evermore,
Brimmed with your rain, on others I o'erflow."

(XXV, 76–78)

"His dew" refers to the Hope breathing through the Psalms of David. This fundamental Hope is the one thing that refreshes and brings new life to others, like the rain falling on the thirsty earth.

Finally, the even more brilliant light which is St. John approaches the poet, and Dante gazes with eager curiosity into the heart of it, wondering if the belief about John's not having died in the body is true. Suddenly he finds that he is blinded by excess of light and that he can no longer see Beatrice at all, and he is in great fear when he realizes that at this high point his vision has failed. St. John speaks to him severely, yet reassuringly, satisfying his curiosity by telling him that only two—Christ and Mary—have entered Heaven with their physical bodies as yet, and adding that the healing eyes of Beatrice will restore his sight, but only after he has answered the questions about Love. "Thy vision is not dead but overcast." Perhaps it means that as our consciousness expands and our vision deepens there is danger that a curious probing into some lesser matter may dangerously distract us from the central experience of Love. It is a crucial moment for Dante, and he is forced to stand in the dark and look wholly inward as he declares the beginning and end of all his Faith and Hope, which is Love.

As Faith is beyond faith and doubt, as Hope is beyond hope and despair, so Love is beyond love and hate. The pendulum may still swing on many levels, but the still point from which it swings is that Love which is Alpha and Omega.

So Dante answers, accepting his blindness with complete faith and certain hope in the love of Beatrice:

> . . . "Swiftly or slowly, as she will,
> May she restore these eyes, that were the gates
> She entered with the fire that burns me still."
>> (XXVI, 13–15)

Barbara Reynolds comments: "Here, the reminder of the first vision of the beauty of Beatrice takes us back to the source of all Dante's experience of love, an experience he does not reject or consider replaced in any way, but now at last followed aright to where it first directed him"[36]—that is, to the One who is beginning and end. Human reason and revelation from the beyond, Dante continues (the voices of conscious and unconscious, we might say), have since that first vision guided his loves. The implication seems to be that if we are aware of the truth at the meeting point of conscious and unconscious, reason and revelation, our love must inevitably seek God who is the source and end of all. If we reject the battle for this ultimate truth, then the arrows of love will fly to secondary targets and be simply one side of the love-hate of instinctive desires. In terms of our day-to-day lives this means the constant effort of maintaining contact with inner and outer truth, so that our choices remain conscious when we are torn between this desire and that.

St. John is not satisfied, as St. Peter was not satisfied, with general ideas. He, too, brings Dante down to brass tacks:

". . . Show by thy words how many are
The teeth whereby this love of thine doth bite."
(XXVI, 50–51)

Love has teeth. It bites, it grips, it tears; it is far from being a nice warm emotion. The phrase brings back those other words of St. Ignatius of Antioch on his way to be thrown to the lions: "Let me be ground by the teeth of the wild beasts that I may become a pure bread." Dante replies with the same image. Literally translated he says, "All those tooth bites which can turn the heart to God have worked together on my love." Love dismembers before it makes whole.

"The being of the world and my own state,
The death He died that I might live the more,
The hope in which I, by faith, participate,

The living truth which I conveyed before,
Have dredged me from the sea of wrongful love
And of the right have set me on the shore.

And through the garden of the world I rove,
Enamoured of its leaves in measure solely
As God the Gardener nurtures them above."
(XXVI, 58–66)

The literal translation of "living truth" is "living consciousness." With these glowing lines Dante ends his definition of his awareness of Love. Once again he leaves us not with a concept but with an image. Faith is a flame, Hope is refreshing rain, and Love unites earth and heaven in the ancient symbols of the garden and the One Gardener.

Now his blindness is dissipated by Beatrice's "radiant gaze," and Dante sees with a new clarity. A fourth light has joined the other three, and this is the soul of Adam, the First Ancestor, the image of fallen man redeemed, who says, as many souls have done, that he can read in the mind of God all the questions that Dante is wishing to ask, "in which all things their perfect image show, yet which in naught its perfect image has." This is the equivalent of the wisdom expressed in the East by "Thou are that; yet is this not thou."

Adam goes on to say that the actual eating of the fruit of the knowledge of good and evil was not the cause of the Fall; it was brought about solely by the "transgression from the path," literally the "passing over the mark." The implication is that man would in any case have grown into the knowledge of evil when his nature became mature enough, but that Eve's haste to know it before the appointed time caused the banishment from Eden and the split whereby man had to learn the nature of evil "by participation" instead of "by understanding," in Barbara Reynold's words. Charles Williams has written of this in *He Came Down from Heaven*. In effect this passage is a firm assertion of the reality of evil and gives the lie to the doctrine of the *privatio boni*, which Dante earlier seems to accept on the intellectual level.

In canto XIX, Dante said the same thing of Lucifer's fall:

> ". . . he fell anon,
> Unripe, because he would not wait for light. . . ."
> (XIX, 47–48)

That is to say, somewhat startlingly, that the original sin from which the disobedience sprang was haste, and that the knowledge of evil was not in itself forbidden. "I must have what I want *now*." Haste is born with the ego's consciousness of time. When a child begins to hurry after a conscious goal, innocence is left behind. This has nothing to do with questions of temperament—a quick, impatient person is not necessarily less mature than a slow, plodding one (the latter may be "hastening" frantically away from responsibility). The waiting which Adam and Eve, and Lucifer himself, refused lies much deeper than this pair of opposites—and the return to it is the life-long task of discriminating patience from cowardice and inertia, creative movement from impatient driving towards a goal. The frenetic hurry which dominates the lives of people in our society, and particularly all the quick ways to psychic health which are so eagerly pursued, take on an even more ominous significance in the light of Dante's words. We are cast out from Eden; and not until our choices are based, not on haste to arrive or to obtain, but on that which has been called by the Chinese the Tao, by the Japanese Zen, by the Indians the Atman, by Jung the Self, by Christians the Will of God, shall we begin to know the Garden of Dante's image, tended by the Gardener and growing in the fullness of time to fruition under sun and rain.

The final episode in the eighth heaven is St. Peter's terrifying denunciation of Pope Boniface VIII referred to earlier, when Dante sees the entire heaven and all the saints including Beatrice suffused with fiery red in sympathy. Boniface and other avaricious, self-seeking, war-mongering Popes have despicably betrayed the meaning of their office—which is, for Catholics, the symbol of the eternal presence of Christ on earth. The world is in terrible disorder as a consequence, but St. Peter predicts a savior, a redeemer, whose coming will not be long delayed, and who will restore the divine order. Beatrice confirms this on the threshold of the Primum Mobile.

It is not difficult to see the inner meaning of this projection from the unconscious of belief in the coming of one who will restore the world to innocence and peace. It has continually broken out into collective consciousness in varying forms. From the expectations of the second coming so prevalent in the past to the quick solutions of all kinds which delude our society today, all are based on this certainty which lies in the unconscious of all of us, of a redemption, a resolution of all conflict which is just around the corner if only we could discover the way to it. Hence the mass hypnosis which Hitler achieved; hence the case with which any psychic panacea can capture thousands of adherents overnight, if only it looks easy enough.

When a certainty of this kind is universally present, it is not proved illusory by the constantly repeated failure of its manifestations. On the contrary, it is most surely an archetype, a basic element of human nature, and therefore a truth of the psyche. All of us, if we are conscious enough, are aware of this feeling within us that we have only to find the key and our conflicts would be over *now*. It is the intuition of that wholeness which is indeed forever there but from which we are cut off by the split in the psyche. Redemption is the conscious discovery of that wholeness, and the more we realize that the redeemer cannot any longer be looked for without, in any sort of projection, the nearer we shall be to the discovery of him in the individual soul. It is astounding how easily Christians have forgotten Christ's absolutely clear teaching on this point.

Here in the eighth heaven, before he passes on to the final vision, to the place of the source of all movement, the Primum Mobile, and then beyond time to the Empyrean, Dante still holds, in the story, to the promise of a new savior in the outer world. In the Primum Mobile and the Empyrean he is to come finally to the resolution of all the opposites in his soul. The tremendous words of Job may stand at this transition point. "For I know that my redeemer liveth, and that he shall stand at the latter day upon the earth: And though after my skin, worms destroy this body, yet in my flesh shall I see God" (Job 19: 25–6).

Before they move on, Dante with his heightened vision looks down and sees below him the seven planets moving on their courses and the earth beneath them. He smiles at its insignificance, and it is no longer the center of the universe to his inner eye, in spite of pre-Copernican astronomy. This is an image, surely, of his new contemplative objectivity—his realization of the smallness of ego-consciousness in the transcendent immensity of the Self. Inevitably we think of the actual experience of the astronauts today, seeing the earth just as did Dante in his vision, as a small sphere in the depths of space. For those of them who are poets at heart, what a tremendous experience it must be.

The Primum Mobile

"The nature of the universe which stills
The centre and revolves all else, from here,
As from its starting-point, all movement wills.

This heaven it is which has no other 'where'
Than the Divine Mind; 'tis but in that Mind
That love, its spur, and the power it rains inhere."

(XXVII, 106–111)

THUS BEATRICE describes this place of the angelic orders. Dante sees a light reflected in her eyes; and, turning, he, like Julian of Norwich, sees God "in a point."

One Point I saw, so radiantly bright,
So searing to the eyes it strikes upon,
They needs must close before such piercing light.

(XXVIII, 16–18)

Around this Point of intense light there revolve nine circles—the nine orders of the angels. "From this Point," says Beatrice, "hang the heavens and all nature." They have their root here, she adds, like a plant in a pot. It reminds one of Ygdrasil, the world tree of Norse mythology, growing downward with its roots in heaven. The Point is indeed the only symbol through which the human imagination can contemplate the Godhead; the point, timeless and without extension, which is nevertheless everywhere and in every moment. This, however, is still only a glimpse and not the final state of awareness of the last canto.

Meanwhile Beatrice expounds to him the function and nature of the Angels and their relationship to the circling of the universe. She enumerates the nine hierarchies of these celestial beings, who are traditionally the powers and intelligences whereby the operations of the divine order are transmitted to

Fig. 42: Heaven of the Primum Mobile

the universe and to man. Their sonorous names derive from St. Paul and from Jewish apocalyptic writings, and the very sound of them quickens the imagination—Seraphim, Cherubim, Thrones, Dominions, Virtues, Powers, Principalities, Archangels, Angels. If, however, we are to feel these beings as actualities in our individual lives, then we must turn to another idiom. When we say that the state of consciousness depends on our relationship to the archetypes in the unconscious, we are in fact reinterpreting the age-old symbol of the Angels whose hidden operations brought either wisdom and protection, or, through the fallen angels, danger of possession by the dark side of these powers.

Perhaps then we may say that the Angels are the powers and intelligence behind the archetypes; and the fact that all the gods and goddesses of the ancient world had their animal counterparts is an image of the twin nature of this world. The animal is a symbol of the subhuman instinctive power in the unconscious; the god figure is the numinous superhuman "intelligence" of the archetypal energy. It remains for man to make conscious, to unite in his own individual being, these two aspects of creation. Only then does he remember himself as he truly is, for though "a little lower than the angels," he, and not they, were created specifically in the image of God. The great danger into which humanity falls is symbolized by the split in the angelic world. When man succumbs to the temptation to invoke one aspect of the archetype without the other, the power without the intelligence, or the intelligence without the power, he is heading for disaster.

Here I will quote some passages from Charles Williams' novel, *The Place of the Lion*, which is concerned with precisely this split. The animal aspects of the angels are loose in a certain village in England and are beginning to destroy all those who have already half-surrendered to the power of the unconscious "pattern of behavior" that each represents. The great numinous beasts are roaming the countryside. (A poison-pen writer is devoured by the snake, an angry man by the lion, etc.) Anthony, who is on the verge of a great breakthrough of individual insight, is told by Richardson, a man who had reached a high order of consciousness, about a text entitled *De Angelis*, written by a scholar of the 16th century whose ideas came from a lost Greek source of the 12th century. Richardson comments, "What is interesting is that it seems to confirm the idea that there was another view of angels from that ordinarily accepted." He goes on to quote from the text, speaking of the "dragon cast out from heaven": ". . . this dragon . . . is accompanied by a ninefold order of spectres, according to the hierarchy of the composed wonders of heaven. . . . and these spectres being invoked have power over those who adore them, and transform them into their very terrible likeness, destroying them with great moanings; as they do also such as inadvisedly set themselves in the way of such powers, wandering without guide or intelligential knowledge, and being made the prey of the uncontrolled emanations."[37] How reminiscent this is of Blake, whose specters and emanations have much the same flavor!

Richardson continues, "The idea seems to be that the energies of these orders can exist in separation from the intelligence which is in them in heaven; and that if deliberately or accidentally you invoke the energy without the intelligence, you're likely eventually to be pretty considerably done for."[38] Examples of this invocation of the powers in the unconscious, "without guide or intelligential knowledge" are plentiful nowadays, but few seem to recognize the danger for what it is. The substitution of psychological terms for symbolic names, while bringing increase of intellectual understanding, can easily rob us of the awe which Dante described on the shores of Purgatory, falling on his knees before the beauty and terror of the Angel. Instead, we either fall prey to the beasts or take refuge in the opposite and equally deadly invocation of the intelligences without the powers—mouthing abstractions and theories and pushing the beasts down again into the unconscious.

The text continues, "For albeit those who paint upon parchment or in churches or make mosaic work of precious metals have designed these holy Universals in human shape, presenting them as youths of beautiful appearance, clothed in candid vestures, and this for the indoctrination of the vulgar . . . yet it is not to be held by the wise that such human masculinities are in any way even a convenient signification of their true nature; nay, those presentations do in some sense darken the true seeker and communicate confusion. . . . For what can the painting of a youth show of these Celestial Benedictions, of which the first circle is that of a lion, and the second circle is that of a serpent, and the third circle is—" "The next eight pages are missing," says Richardson. Then later there is a passage of special interest to us. "For though these nine zones are divided into a trinity of trinities, yet after another fashion there are four without and four within, and between them is the Glory of the Eagle. For this is he who knows both himself, and the others, and is their own knowledge; as it is written *We shall know as we are known*—this is the knowledge of the Heavenly Ones, and it is called the Virtue of the Celestials. . . . As it is written *The Lord brought you out of Egypt on the back of a strong eagle*."[39] We may be reminded of Gwaihir the Windlord in Tolkien's *Lord of the Rings*, three times the rescuer of those who had done battle with the Dragon.

Man, it is implied at the end of the text, has dominion over the beast only when he has found, become conscious of, the Sacred Eagle; and we remember Dante's Eagle in the Heaven of Jupiter, speaking the unity of the many and the one. Finally Richardson warns again of the ease with which we allow conventional pictures and ideas of subtle sweetness to influence us. The Angels, he says, are rather "the principles of the tiger, and the volcano and the flaming suns of space."[40]

Principles they may symbolize; but for Dante, as always, abstractions are meaningless. For him, every single Angel (and their number, says Beatrice, is past imagining) differs from all the others, just as every human being is unique; and God's light is reflected in each one differently.

> "The Primal Light the whole irradiates,
> And is received therein as many ways
> As there are splendours wherewithal it mates.
>
> . . . .
>
> Consider well the breadth, behold the height
> Of His eternal Goodness, seeing that o'er
> So many mirrors It doth shed Its light,
>
> Yet One abideth as It was before."
>
> (XXIX, 136–145)

Each man's relationship to the Angels, therefore, is not just an attitude to a principle. It is for each a unique meeting with the unconscious through specific images and experiences which personify for him the "powers and intelligences" at the roots of being, under both their aspects of creation and destruction. Very often we meet the Angels in our dreams without recognizing them.

Halfway through her conversation about the Angels, Beatrice has paused "To gaze, with rapturous and smiling mien, full on the Point" which is God. She then speaks to Dante about the Creation, seeing his longing to know the origin of time and space. She explains that Eternal Love brought all creation into being instantaneously outside time.

> "Not to increase His good, which cannot be,
> But that His splendour, shining back, might say:
> *Behold, I am*, in His eternity. . . ."
>
> (XXIX, 13–15)

In other words, through the creation God became conscious of Himself. "In the beginning was the Word," when God was able to say, "I am." So also man, made in His image, can truly say, "I am," only when he, in his sphere, however simple and undramatic, has become an individual creator.

The Empyrean

THE RINGS OF angelic light have faded one by one, and Dante, looking upon Beatrice's radiant beauty, now intensified past all description, is told by her that they are in the Empyrean. All sense of motion is left behind; we do not travel *towards* eternity. Dante is aware of a new power of seeing, a new state of consciousness leading beyond becoming to being:

> Light I beheld which as a river flowed,
> Fulgid with splendour; and on either shore
> The colours of a wondrous springtime showed.
>
> And from the stream arose a glittering store
> Of living sparks which, winging mid the blooms,
> To rubies set in gold resemblance bore.
>   (XXX, 61–66)

Beatrice, however, tells him that these images are still merely "shadow-prefaces" of the truth, geared to the immaturity still remaining in his vision. He must now drink of this great river of light—drink with his eyes here on this threshold, as he had drunk with his mouth of Lethe and Eunoe in that other, Earthly Paradise. Drinking and looking have become one.

> No little infant mouths as readily
> Towards his mother's breast, if he awake
> Much later than his hour is wont to be,
>
> As mirrors of mine eyes I then did make,
> In eagerness inclining o'er the stream. . . .
>   (XXX, 82–86)

So, in another of his supremely simple images, does Dante tie the end to the beginning—the unconsciously innocent hunger

Fig. 43: The Empyrean

of the tiny child to the recovered innocence of the conscious man on the threshold of enlightenment.

> And as these eyelids drank unto their brim,
> Beneath my gaze the river's contours swayed,
> Spreading and curving to a circle's rim.
>
> As people sporting in a masquerade,
> When they put off disguising semblances,
> Altered, yet as they are, then stand displayed. . . .
>
> (XXX, 88–93)

The straight lines of life in time, the rivers flowing from place to place, are stripped of their "disguising semblances," the masquerade of temporal cause and effect, and seen in their true form as the circle of eternity—"altered, yet as they are." And now the *lumen gloriae*, the light of glory, is revealed to him as an immense white rose.

> Splendour of God, whereby these eyes beheld
> Thy true realm's triumph, grant me power to say
> How that exalted triumph I beheld.
>
> In yonder heaven the *lumen gloriae*
> Reveals the Maker to created mind
> Which in His sight alone finds peace for aye.
>
> . . . .

As water by a mountain's foot may be
A glass wherein it sees itself so fair,
Decked out in grass and flowers luxuriantly,

So, mirrored in that light, tier upon tier,
On myriad thrones, rising on every side.
Those who from here returned I gazed on there.

If in its inmost petals can reside
So vast a light, in such a rose as this
What width immense must in the rim abide?

My sight, being undismayed, ne'er went amiss
In all that amplitude and height, but knew
The full extent and nature of such bliss.

For "near" and "far" no reckoning is due,
Since nothing by the law of nature goes
Where God no agents needs His will to do.

      (XXX, 97–123)

How often the vivid, earthy images recur here in the topmost heaven—the hungry baby, the masqueraders, the lake at the mountain's foot. Like strong buttresses rooted in the ground, they carry, as it were, the weight of so much soaring splendor.

Standing in the "gold of the eternal rose," that is, in the yellow center with the white petals unfolding around him, Dante sees the souls of those who have "returned" to conscious innocence, and sees them no longer as lights or flames or jewels or hazy faces (as in the moon) but clearly in their human forms. Among the angels.

As bees ply back and forth, now in the flowers
Busying themselves, and now intent to wend
Where all their toil is turned to sweetest stores,

So did the host of Angels now descend
Amid the Flower of the countless leaves,
Now rise to where their love dwells without end.

      (XXXI, 7–13)

"The Flower of the countless leaves"—symbol in all ages and all places of the Whole—Dante's white rose, the golden flower of the Chinese, the thousand-petalled lotus of India.

I, coming to holiness from the profane,
To the eternal from the temporal,
From Florence to a people just and sane,

Into what stupor, then, must I needs fall!
Truly, 'twixt it and joy I then preferred
No sound to hear, no word to speak at all.

(XXXI, 37–42)

He turns in his stupor to Beatrice once more; but Beatrice has
gone, and in her place stands an old man. It is St. Bernard, the
saint who of all others is distinguished by his devotion to the
Mother of God. Like Dante himself, he had been led all his life
long by his vision of the Lady of his soul; and now it is he
who will initiate Dante into his final illumination.

Dante's vision here again accords with Jung's knowledge
of the unconscious. After the assimilation of the anima comes
the leadership of the "wise old man"; and when the archetype
of the Self appears in human form, the image is almost always
of the same sex as the dreamer. The guide to the inner world
is of the opposite sex; the anima in man or the animus in
woman is the link between the personal world and the archetypal depths, and they lead us down into the pits of Hell and
up the holy mountain to that which is beyond. I am not
forgetting Virgil. He was the actual companion on the first
stage; but he was sent by Beatrice, and of her guidance we are
constantly reminded. This too, I believe, is true to our experience. Without the awakening of the sense of relatedness (the
feminine value) in man, or the discrimination of an inner goal
(the masculine value) in woman, no one could start on the
way; nevertheless, the leading of the animus and anima must
be mediated through the most conscious human qualities of
each one's own sex principle. Here on the last threshold,
however, Beatrice gives place to Bernard, through whom Dante
will pass for an instant beyond all images to the whole.

Beatrice does not simply disappear. She goes from Dante's
personal presence to her place in the eternal Rose. She is
infinitely remote now, and yet more distinctly visible to him
than ever before (since in this place, "for 'near' and 'far' no
reckoning is due").

And there I saw her in her glory crowned,
Reflecting from herself the eternal rays.

The greatest height whence thunderings resound
Less distant is for mortal vision, though
Plunged in the deepest ocean it were found,

Than was my sight from Beatrice, and lo!
By no material means made visible,
Distinct her image came to me below.

(XXXI, 71–78)

There are no tears here, as at the parting with Virgil. For Dante now, the personal separation is known as unity, and his heart cries out in gratitude:

"O thou in whom my hopes securely dwell,
And who, to bring my soul to Paradise,
Didst leave the imprint of thy steps in Hell,

Of all that I have looked on with these eyes
Thy goodness and thy power have fitted me
The holiness and grace to recognize.

Thou hast led me, a slave, to liberty,
By every path, and using every means
Which to fulfil this task were granted thee.

Keep turned towards me thy munificence
So that my soul which thou hast remedied
May please thee when it quits the bonds of sense."

Such was my prayer and she, so distant fled,
It seemed, did smile and look on me once more,
Then to the eternal fountain turned her head.

The holy elder spoke. . . .

(XXXI, 79—94)

Here, as we leave her, it is as it was on her first meeting with Dante after his parting from Virgil; Beatrice is looking away from him at the center. But what an immense difference there is in Dante himself! There, we remember, he sees her gaze fixed on a theriomorphic image which he can only conceive of as half this and half that, or alternately of one nature or the other; and his one hope is to keep his eyes fixed on hers. Here, as she turns those eyes finally to the "eternal fountain," he can let her go, for his own journey is drawing, as St. Bernard tells him, to its close in immediate vision.

First he directs Dante to look upon The Lady herself. No one, man or woman, can see God unless he has first seen the Mother of God in her human form as Queen of Heaven; there can be no bypassing of the humanity through which God gives birth to Himself.

> I looked above and, as the orient scene
> At dawn exceeds the beauty of the west,
> Where the declining sun has lately been,
>
> So, mounting as from vale to mountain-crest,
> These eyes beheld, at the remotest rim,
> A radiance surpassing all the rest.
>
> . . . .
>
> About the heart I saw on outstretched wing
> More than a thousand angels jubilant,
> Distinct in radiance and in functioning.
>
> (XXXI, 118–132)

Here Dante again insists that each of those myriad Angels is *distinct* both in his essence and in his action. Immediately we are again saved from imagining all this joy as a blaze of undifferentiated light.

In the next, the penultimate canto, St. Bernard points out many of the individual souls and resolves some last confusions about predestination. In another of his down-to-earth images, Dante says of divine grace that "as men's hair of divers shades doth grow" so is the grace of God different in its operation for each individual. It is the paradox first expounded by Piccarda in the heaven of the Moon and remaining to the end something the intellect can never comprehend, though it can be satisfied when thought is united to vision. The whole canto is a further insistence, before the final awareness breaks through, of the "pattern of the glory" (Charles Williams). Barbara Reynolds writes, "In the almost rigid precision and symmetry of the ranks of the blessed, the perfection of the divine order is conveyed. God's plan for mankind, His heavenly kingdom, are as satisfying to the intellect as a geometrical design."[41]

And so we come to the final canto which opens with St. Bernard's prayer to the Virgin. The first line is that great and gloriously simple phrase which encompasses all reality in six words:

Vergine Madre, figlia del tuo figlio, . . .
(Virgin Mother, daughter of your son)

> (XXXIII, 1)

And St. Bernard continues:

Thou art that She by whom our human nature
Was so ennobled that it might become
The Creator to create Himself His creature.

> (XXXIII, 4–6)

The literal translation of this is: "Thou art she who so ennobled human nature that its own maker did not scorn to become a thing made by this nature." This truly is a statement, as far as words can possibly define it, of the *conjunctio* of God with an "ennobled," or, we should say, conscious humanity, which Dante is to know by direct experience.

This experience, however, cannot come to any one man until he has penetrated into another mystery. Who was it who said that there can be in one sense no private individual salvation? No one man is whole unless he knows all humanity as whole in that instant. This profundity is symbolized here by St. Bernard's prayer to the Virgin (who *is* all humanity) to intercede for Dante, that he may know "the final source." In this prayer every soul in the white rose joins; and St. Bernard hints at the essential condition of the ultimate union in his words, "This man, who witnessed from the deepest pit of all the universe, up to this height, the souls' lives one by one" (the words are, in fact, "the deepest *lake*"). Without the descent into the water, without the individual discrimination ("the souls' lives one by one"), there is no ascent, no consciousness of the final sources. The Virgin answers St. Bernard by simply raising her eyes to the eternal light.

And I, who now was drawing ever nigher
Towards the end of yearning, as was due,
Quenched in my soul the burning of desire.
. . . .

For now my sight, clear and yet clearer grown,
Pierced through the ray of that exalted light,
Wherein, as in itself, the truth is known.

Henceforth my vision mounted to a height
Where speech is vanquished and must lag behind,
And memory surrenders in such plight.

As from a dream one may awake to find
Its passion yet imprinted on the heart,
Although all else is cancelled from the mind,

So of my vision now but little part
Remains, yet in my inmost soul I know
The sweet instilling which it did impart.

(XXXIII, 46–63)

"O Light supreme," prays Dante, "make strong my tongue that in its words may burn one single spark of all Thy glory's light. . . ." He then tells us that he knew suddenly that if he had in that supreme experience turned away his eyes, even for an instant, he would have been lost; and this thought gave him courage to penetrate deeper and deeper until his gaze was united with the "infinite value." As in this ultimate moment, so at every new insight along the way, these words carry wisdom for each of us. When the strong light of a numinous image breaks through, all too often we fail to find the courage to stay with it by continuing to *look at it* and to bear the piercing of the new light until our gaze penetrates to the value. A dream whose "passion is imprinted on the heart" is quickly forgotten even after discussion of it, and we cannot too often remember how easily the passion may be swamped by trivialities. We all have a very hard time remembering Jung's strong assertion that it is not our understanding of the meaning of a dream, important though our effort to find it may be, which changes us, but the intensity of our response to the images in our hearts and minds—the refusal, indeed, to look away from them. If we do so look away, then very quickly they become a "nothing but" experience. It was Dante's sense of this danger which gave him, he says, the boldness to gaze deeper and deeper.

O grace abounding, whereby I presumed
So deep the eternal light to search and sound
That my whole vision was therein consumed!

In that abyss I saw how love held bound
Into one volume all the leaves whose flight
Is scattered through the universe around. . . .
(XXXIII, 82–87)

After some more lines about the identity of the many and
the one which he saw in "that abyss" and of the transformation
he felt within himself, Dante launches into an attempt to
convey in images his vision of the Trinity.

That light supreme, within its fathomless
Clear substance, showed to me three spheres, which bare
Three hues distinct, and occupied one space;

The first mirrored the next, as though it were
Rainbow from rainbow, and the third seemed flame
Breathed equally from each of the first pair.

How weak are words, and how unfit to frame
My concept—which lags after what was shown
So far, 'twould flatter it to call it lame!
(XXXIII, 115–123)

And now, in the last twenty-one lines of the poem, comes
Dante's supreme realization of the fourth and of the union of
this fourth with the three in the final totality. The image of the
fourth for Dante is our human form itself, which he sees deep
in the circle which is the Son of God. At this, Dante's sight,
his eyes, are altogether absorbed into the vision. Since the
word used is *viso*, which more often means "face" than "gaze,"
we could say his own individual inmost form was so absorbed,
while yet remaining itself.

Eternal light, that in Thyself alone
Dwelling, alone dost know Thyself, and smile
On Thy self-love, so knowing and so known!

The sphering thus begot, perceptible
In Thee like mirrored light, now to my view—
When I had looked on it a little while—

Seemed in itself, and in its own self-hue,
Limned with our image; for which cause mine eyes
Were altogether drawn and held thereto.
(XXXIII, 124–132)

As has been pointed out by Emma Jung and M. L. von Franz in their book on the Grail legend (p. 341), the image of Mary, of humanity itself, as the fourth in the quaternity of the Godhead does not mean that the problem of evil has been evaded; for everything human, all earthly reality is both dark and light, evil and good. Early Christianity could not accept any hint of darkness in God; hence the extreme emphasis on the sinlessness of both Mary and her Son. Nevertheless, no amount of insistence can destroy the facts of their human confrontation with evil—their freedom to choose. Mary *could* have refused the message of the Angel; Jesus *could* have fallen to the devil's temptation. Once we deny that, the whole meaning of the Incarnation disappears. If they were subject to temptation at all, then in common with all men evil was a reality within them as in us; and in their flesh they are taken into Heaven. What is happening today is not the end of Christianity, but the discovery of that fourth which has always been implicit in it, and which has been seen and experienced intuitively by individuals all through the centuries, as here, in his supreme moment, by Dante himself.

The fourth, then, is humanity with all its potential light and darkness (*not*, be it always remembered, the personal ego) seen now by Dante in the heart of the Godhead. But still he sees this human image as something superimposed on the eternal circle; he has not yet *realized* the two as one; and still therefore, being Dante, while holding his gaze steady with all the intense feeling of his heart, he strives with every power of his mind to understand.

> As the geometer his mind applies
> To square the circle, not for all his wit
> Finds the right formula, howe'er he tries,
>
> So strove I with that wonder—how to fit
> The image to the sphere; so sought to see
> How it maintained the point of rest in it.
>
> (XXXIII, 133–138)

The problem of squaring the circle[42] was not proved impossible until much later, but Dante already in the *Convivio* had said it was insoluble. It is a symbol of the attempt to equate the square of the earth and time to the circle of heaven and eternity—and the tools of man's intellect are useless before this final mystery. Nevertheless they must be used to the uttermost.

We come to the last seven lines of the poem. I will quote here first Barbara Reynolds' and then John Ciardi's[43] beautiful rendering:

> Thither my own wings could not carry me,
> But that a flash my understanding clove,
> Whence its desire came to it suddenly.
>
> High phantasy lost power and here broke off;
> Yet, as a wheel moves smoothly, free from jars,
> My will and my desire were turned by love,
>
> The love that moves the sun and the other stars.

* * * * * * *

> But mine were not the wings for such a flight.
> Yet, as I wished, the truth I wished for came
> Cleaving my mind in a great flash of light.
>
> Here my powers rest from their high fantasy,
> But already I could feel my being turned—
> Instinct and intellect balanced equally
>
> As in a wheel whose motion nothing jars
> By the love that moves the sun and the other stars.
>
> (XXXIII, 139–145)

It is a curious fact that almost everyone who knows anything at second hand about Dante has heard that exceedingly famous last line, but that very few are aware of the two preceding lines (three in Ciardi's version) which give the line the tremendous meaning it carries. By itself it is a statement that love is the center of the universe and of all creation. In its context it recalls the entire meaning of Dante's journey from dark wood to white rose, and beyond.

Maybe it is not so strange that men quote it out of context. Hearing the line alone we may know aesthetically its beauty and truth and react with awe; but if we have the courage to be wholly aware of it in its context, here at the journey's end, then we are irrevocably involved. For Dante's journey is ours, and we too descend into Hell; we too struggle up the mountain

Fig. 44: The Empyrean

of consciousness and must pass through fire and water until we dare to face the responsibilities of joy. Thus the way is complete in that final wheeling of desire and will, instinct and intellect, flesh and spirit, moved only by the center which is Love.

> ma non eran da ciò le proprie penne:
> se non che la mia mente fu percossa
> da un fulgore, in che sua voglia venne.
>
> A l'alta fantasia qui mancò possa;
> ma già volgeva il mio disio e 'l velle
> sì come rota ch'igualmente è mossa,
>
> l'amor che move il sole e l'altre stelle.
>
> (XXXIII, 139–145)

Notes

[1] Lewis, C. S., *The Problem of Pain* (New York: Macmillan, 1944), pp. 103–104.

[2] Williams, Charles, *The Figure of Beatrice* (New York: Noonday Press, 1961), p. 11.

[3] Sayers, Dorothy, *The Comedy of Dante Alighieri, Cantica I, Hell* (London/Baltimore: Penguin Books, 1949), p. 121.

[4] Sayers, *Hell*, p. 269.

[5] *Ibid.*

[6] *Ibid.*, p. 275.

[7] Sayers, Dorothy, *The Comedy of Dante Alighieri, Cantica II, Purgatory* (London/Baltimore: Penguin Books, 1955), p. 19.

[8] *Ibid.*, pp. 17–18.

[9] Von Franz, Marie Louise, *Introduction to the Psychology of Fairy Tales* (New York: Spring Publications, 1970), chap. VII, p. 12.

[10] *The Woman Who Could Not Die* by Julia de Beausobre (London: Victor Gollancz Ltd., 1948).

[11] Sayers, *Purgatory*, p. 122.

[12] *Ibid.*, p. 140.

[13] *Ibid.*, p. 209.

[14] *Ibid.*, p. 220.

[15] Jung, writing about alchemical symbolism, says: "Nor is realization through feeling the final stage. Although it does not really belong to this chapter, yet it might not be out of place to mention the fourth stage after the three already discussed, particularly since it has such a very pronounced symbolism in alchemy. This fourth stage is the anticipation of the lapis (the stone, the Self). The imaginative activity of the fourth function—intuition, without which no realization is complete—is plainly evidenced in this anticipation of a possibility whose fulfillment could never be the object of empirical experience at all. . . . Intuition gives outlook and insight; it revels in the garden of magical possibilities as if they were real. . . . This keystone rounds off the work into an experience of the totality of the individual. Such an experience is completely foreign to our age, although no previous age has ever needed wholeness as much" ("The Psychology of Transference," in *The Practice of Psychotherapy*, Second Edition, New York: Pantheon, 1966, p. 281).

[16] Jung, C. G., "The Love Problem of a Student," in *Civilization in Transition*, Collected Works, Vol. 10 (New York: Pantheon Books, 1964), pp. 111–112.

[17] Jung, C. G., *Memories, Dreams, Reflections* (New York: Pantheon Books, 1963), p. 35.

[18] Sayers, *Purgatory*, p. 267.

[19] *Ibid.*, pp. 302–303.

[20] *Ibid.*, p. 312.

[21] Sayers, Dorothy, *Essays Presented to Charles Williams* (Oxford University Press, 1947), pp. 3–4.

[22] Lewis, C. S., *Till We Have Faces* (New York: Harcourt, Brace and World, 1956), p. 306.

[23] Sayers, Dorothy L., and Reynolds, Barbara, *The Comedy of Dante Alighieri, Cantica III, Paradise* (London/Baltimore: Penguin Books, 1962), pp. 31–32.

[24] *Ibid.*, p. 16.

[25] Eliot, T. S., *Dante* (London: Faber and Faber, 1929), pp. 49 and 45.

[26] Jung, C. G., "The Psychology of Transference," in *The Practice of Psychotherapy*, Collected Works, Vol. 16, Second Edition (New York: Pantheon, 1966), p. 305.

[27] Jaffe, A., *From the Life and Works of C.G. Jung*, (New York: Harper and Row, Colophon Books, 1971), p. 42.

[28] Sayers and Reynolds, p. 140.

[29] The actuality of this is, of course, in the dogma, still projected into the future, and Dante is simply given the grace to see them as they will be.

[30] Sayers and Reynolds, p. 237.

[31] Adler, G., "On the Question of Meaning," in *The Well Tended Tree* (New York: Putnam, 1971), p. 160.

[32] *Ibid.*

[33] Krishnamurti, *Freedom from the Known* (New York: Harper and Row), p. 70.

[34] *Ibid.*, p. 31.

[35] Sanford, John, "Analytical Psychology: Science and Religion," In *The Well Tended Tree* (New York: Putnam, 1971), p. 99.

[36] Sayers and Reynolds, p. 287.

[37] Williams, Charles, *The Place of the Lion* (London: Faber and Faber, 1952), pp. 90–92.

[38] *Ibid.*

[39] *Ibid.*, pp. 90–93.

[40] *Ibid.*, p. 94.

[41] Sayers and Reynolds, p. 338.

[42] "The problem loosely described as 'squaring the circle' is stated by Dante with his usual accuracy. The radius and circumference of a circle being incommensurable it is impossible to express the circumference exactly in terms of the radius" (Temple Classics, Dante, *Paradiso*, p. 409).

[43] Ciardi, John, *Dante's Paradiso* (New York: The New American Library, 1961), p. 365.

Glossary

AMIMA and ANIMUS: Personifications of the unconscious femininity in the psyche of man and of the unconscious masculinity in the psyche of woman. In her negative form the anima will manifest herself in a man's irrational moods and emotions; the negative animus is made up of a woman's second-hand opinions, sweeping generalizations, and imperatives. Their positive natural function, once we relate to them, is to act as guides to the unconscious and to the creative images within.

ALLEGORY and SYMBOL: Whereas a symbol is the meeting point of conscious and unconscious meanings which awaken in us an awareness of something that cannot be expressed in rational terms, an allegory is merely a representation of conscious abstract ideas.

ARCHETYPE: The archetypes themselves are the indefinable natural forces underlying human life in all ages and all places. They cannot be known directly, but archetypal themes appear all over the world in myth, in fairy tales, fantasies, dreams, etc. We can recognize these archetypal motifs by their fascination, their irrational power to move us. A few of the most frequent archetypal symbols are the hero, the wise old man, the nourishing and devouring mother, the water of life, and so on.

ASSOCIATION: "Mental connection between an object and ideas related to it" (*Oxford English Dictionary*).

CONSCIOUSNESS and the UNCONSCIOUS: The conscious mind contains all that we know, and the ego is the carrier of this knowledge. The unconscious comprises all that we do not know in the inner world, from personal repressions to all the vast possibilities of the psyche, future, and past.

EGO: "The conscious thinking subject" (*Oxford English Dictionary*).

HUBRIS: The Greek word for overweening pride which seeks to usurp the power of the gods. It led to *nemesis*, the vengeance of the gods.

INCUBUS and SUCCUBUS: Medieval terms. The incubus was a male demon who had sexual intercourse with a woman; the succubus a female demon having intercourse with a man.

MANA: A Melanesian word for a supernatural power felt in a person, event, or object.

MANDALA: A "magic" circle, symbolizing psychic totality and expressing the pattern of life around the center. Mandalas are found all over the world. They were used especially in India as "yantras"— aids to contemplation. Their structure is usually based on the number 4 within the circle. Their forms are often variations on the flower, the cross, or the wheel. Traditional mandalas, whether Eastern or Christian, have the Deity at the center. Individuals nowadays often produce mandalas spontaneously from the unconscious, and the center is apt to be a point. They are not consciously contrived patterns.

PROJECTION: Everything of which we are unconscious is "projected" into the outer world, and we see it in events and people outside ourselves. Thus the less conscious we are of our own rejected and inferior qualities and of the realities of the inner world, the less objectivity we have in our judgments of people and things, for they are hidden behind our projections of our unknown selves.

PSYCHE: The psyche is defined in the dictionary as soul, spirit, mind. As used by Jung it includes all the non-physical realities of the human being.

SELF: Jung has used this term to express the idea of the center—the center which is also the circumference—the totality of the personality, embracing all, both consciousness and the unconscious. This center of being has a thousand names: the Atman in India, Christ in Christianity, the stone in alchemy, the diamond, the child, the flower, the circle, the square, the Tao in China. All these are but a few of the symbols through which men have experienced this central mystery of life.

SHADOW: The shadow (in dreams always of the same sex as the dreamer) personifies all the inferior and rejected sides of the personality. These shadow qualities are not all negative, but may also be potentialities for which the ego has not taken responsibility.

SUCCUBUS: See INCUBUS above.

SYMBOL: See ALLEGORY above.

TRANSCENDENT FUNCTION: This is the function which transcends and unites the ordinary functions of the personality. When we experience it, the oppositions of conscious and unconscious, of flesh and spirit, are resolved and the functioning of the ego is in total harmony with the center, the Self, the Will of God.

UNCONSCIOUS: See CONSCIOUSNESS above.

Credits

Special acknowledgement to Peter Brieger, Millard Meiss, and Charles S. Singleton, Illuminated Manuscripts of the Divine Comedy, Bollingen Series LXXXI, Princeton University Press, 1969, from which these manuscript paintings (with the exception of the cover) were selected. Special thanks to Joan Palatine, Permissions Manager, Princeton University Press.

Cover: "Dante and His Poem," by Domenico di Michelino. (Italian, XV cent.) Scala/Art Resource, K26056.

Frontispiece: Florence, Ricc. 1038, 225v (Florentine, 2nd half XV cent.)

Fig. 1: Madrid, B.N. Vit. 23-2, 1v (Florentine, ca. 1415)

Fig. 2: Florence, Ricc. 1035, 4v (Venetian, 2nd quarter XV cent.)

Fig. 3: London, B.M. Yates Thompson 36, 3r (Priamo della Quercia, mid XV cent.) By permission of the British Library.

Fig. 4: Chantilly, Musée Condé 597, 48r (Pisan, ca. 1345). Photograph courtesy Giraudon, Paris.

Fig. 5: Chantilly, Musée Condé 597, 52v (Pisan, ca. 1345). Photograph courtesy Giraudon, Paris.

Fig. 6: Paris, B.N. it. 2017, 71v (Lombard, Vitae Imperatorum Master, ca. 1440)

Fig. 7: Paris, B.N. it. 74, 23v (Bartolomeo di Fruosino, ca. 1420)

Fig. 8: The Pierpont Morgan Library, New York. M. 676 f. 16v (Italian, late XIV cent.)

Fig. 9: London, B.M. Yates Thompson 36, 16r (Priamo della Quercia, mid XV cent.)

Fig. 10: Florence, Ricc. 1035, 20v (Venetian, 2nd quarter XV cent.)

Fig. 11: Holkham Hall 514, p. 19 (Italian, 3rd quarter XIV cent.) By permission of the Bodleian Library.

Fig. 12: London, B.M. Add. 19587, 24v (Neapolitan, ca. 1370) By permission of the British Library.

Fig. 13: The Pierpont Morgan Library, New York. M. 676 f. 27r (Italian, late XIV cent.)

Fig. 14: Holkham Hall 514, p. 28 (Italian, 3rd quarter XIV cent.) By permission of the Bodleian Library.

Fig. 15: Holkham Hall 514, p. 39 (Italian, 3rd quarter XIV cent.) By permission of the Bodleian Library.

Fig. 16: Imola, Com. 32, 21r (Lombard, Vitae Imperatorum Master, ca. 1440)

Fig. 17: London, B.M. Add. 19587, 52v (Neapolitan, ca. 1370) By permission of the British Library.

Fig. 18: Chantilly, Musée Condé 597, 223v (Pisan, ca. 1345) Photograph courtesy Giraudon, Paris.

Fig. 19: London, B.M. Add. 19587, 60r (Neapolitan, ca. 1370) By permission of the British Library.

Fig. 20: Holkham Hall 514, p. 57 (Italian, 3rd quarter XIV cent.) By permission of the Bodleian Library.

Fig. 21: London, B.M. Add. 19587, 63r (Neapolitan, ca. 1370) By permission of the British Library.

Fig. 22: Holkham Hall 514, p. 63 (Italian, 3rd quarter XIV cent.) By permission of the Bodleian Library.

Fig. 23: Holkham Hall 514, p. 73 (Italian, 3rd quarter XIV cent.) By permission of the Bodleian Library.

Fig. 24: Holkham Hall 514, p. 74 (Italian, 3rd quarter XIV cent.) By permission of the Bodleian Library.

Fig. 25: Holkham Hall 514, p. 78 (Italian, 3rd quarter XIV cent.) By permission of the Bodleian Library.

Fig. 26: Holkham Hall 514, p. 93 (Italian, 3rd quarter XIV cent.) By permission of the Bodleian Library.

Fig. 27: Holkham Hall 514, p. 99 (Italian, 3rd quarter XIV cent.) By permission of the Bodleian Library.

Fig. 28: Holkham Hall 514, p. 105 (Italian, 3rd quarter XIV cent.) By permission of the Bodleian Library.

Fig. 29: Padua, Seminario 67, 176r (Paduan, early XV cent.)

Fig. 30: The Pierpont Morgan Library, New York. M. 676 f. 83r (Italian, late XIV cent.)

Fig. 31: London, B.M. Add. 19587, 109v (112v) (Neapolitan, late XIV cent.) By permission of the British Library.

Fig. 32: London, B.M. Egerton 943, 120v (Emilian or Paduan, 2nd quarter XIV cent.) By permission of the British Library.

Fig. 33: The Pierpont Morgan Library, New York. M. 676 f. 89v (Italian, late XIV cent.)

Fig. 34: Paris, Arsenal 8530, 120r (Italian, mid XIV cent.) By permission of the Bibliothèque Nationale.

Fig. 35: Copenhagen, Kgl. Bib. Thott 411.2, 162v (Early XV cent.) Collection of the Royal Library, Copenhagen.

Fig. 36: Copenhagen, Kgl. Bib. Thott 411.2, 183r (Early XV cent.) Collection of the Royal Library, Copenhagen.

Fig. 37: Copenhagen, Kgl. Bib. Thott 411.2, 186v (early XV cent.) Collection of the Royal Library, Copenhagen.

Fig. 38: Paris, Arsenal 8530, 142r (Italian, mid XIV cent.) By permission of the Bibliothèque Nationale.

Fig. 39: London, B.M. Yates Thompson 36, 162r (Giovanni di Paolo, mid XV cent.) By permission of the British Library.

Fig. 40: London, B.M. Yates Thompson 36, 165r (Giovanni di Paolo, mid XV cent.) By permission of the British Library.

Fig 41: London, B.M. Yates Thompson 36, 172r (Giovanni di Paolo, mid XV cent.) By permission of the British Library.

Fig. 42: Florence, Laur. Plut. 40.1, 312v (North Italian, 1456).

Fig 43: London, B.M. Egerton 943, 186r (Emilian or Paduan, 2nd quarter XIV cent.) By permission of the British Library.

Fig 44: London, B.M. Yates Thompson 36, 188r (Giovanni di Paolo, mid XV cent.) By permission of the British Library.